THE HOME
BAKING
BOOK

STEFAN ELIAS

THE HOME BAKING BOOK

TIMELESS RECIPES FOR ARTISANAL TREATS

HANNIBAL

FOREWORD, 9
Stefan Elias

BLOCH, 11

INTRODUCTION, 13
Greet Draye

THE GOLDEN RULES OF BAKING, 20

PASTRY BASICS, 24

GLOSSARY, 32

KITCHEN ESSENTIALS, 34

MORNING ROLLS AND BUNS, 37

- SAVOURY TOPPINGS FOR MORNING OR LUNCHTIME BAGELS, 40
- BOERKES PLAIN, WITH NUTS, SULTANAS, OR CURRANTS (VEGAN), 42
- CRISPY SEEDED OVEN BAGELS (VEGAN), 44
- SOFT ROLLS WITH SUNFLOWER SEEDS AND OMEGA 3 SEED MIX, 46
- PICCOLOS AND BARM CAKES (VEGAN), 48
- SWEET KADETJES (BUNS), 51

SWEET BREAKFAST, 53

- BOULES ALSACIENNES, 54
- CREAM AND CHOCOLATE RONDELETTE, 56
- ALMOND CROISSANT, 57
- GALETTES, 58
- CHERRY CROISSANT, 61
- CHOCOLATE POCHE, 62
- SESAME AND CHOCOLATE VIENNOISE, 64
- ROUND SUISSE WITH RAISINS, 66
- STREUSEL BRIOCHE, 68
- BOURBON VANILLA BRIOCHE, 69
- MARITOZZO, 70
- SUGAR KNOT, 72
- FILLED MASTEL, 76
- CREAM BRIOCHE, 78
- CRUFFINS (VEGAN), 80
- NOISETTE, 83
- SUGAR BOLUS, 84
- BRIOCHE À TÊTE, 86

BREAD AND BUTTER, 89

- BOULDOUK BRIOCHE, 92
- WHOLEMEAL FRUIT AND HAZELNUT LOAF (VEGAN), 94
- VANILLA BOULOT PERLÉ, 96
- SESAME SANDWICH LOAF (VEGAN), 98
- TEAR (AND SHARE) SANDWICH LOAF, 100
- BRIOCHE LOAF WITH CHOCOLATE, 102
- RUSTIC PAIN DE CAMPAGNE/COUNTRY LOAF (VEGAN), 104
- BRIOCHE DE NANTERRE WITH RAISINS, 107
- GALETTE BRIOCHÉE, 108
- SOFT NUT BRETZEL (VEGAN), 111
- COUQUE CHIFFON, 112
- SEMOLINA FALUCHE (VEGAN), 114
- BABKALLAH, 116
- PAGNON AMANDE, 118

ON THE CAKE STAND, 121

- PARIS BREST, 122
- PEAR TARTE TATIN, 125
- CHOCOLATE AND DARK CHERRY CAKE, 126
- GRANDMOTHER'S FLAN CAKE, 128
- SOUTHERN MINI FLAN CAKES, 133
- GOURMAND FLAN CAKE, 134
- SUMMER FRUIT CAKE, 136
- CHEESECAKE, 138
- WALNUT CHAGALL, 140
- LUXEMBOURGOISE, 142
- PEAR CHARLOTTE CAKE, 144

- CARAMEL CHOCOLATE FUDGE CAKE, 146
- ÉCLAIR PARISIEN, 149
- TEA PIE WITH A SWEET FRUIT FILLING, 150
- CITRONELLA, 152
- CHOUQUETTE, 154
- TARTELETTE MAISON, 157
- NUT TARTLET, 158
- THE TASTIEST CARROT CAKE, 160
- BUDINI DI RISO, 162

DELICIOUS FRUIT PIES, 165

- APPLE PIE ALSACIENNE, 167
- CHERRY PIE (VEGAN), 168
- OLD-FASHIONED APPLE PIE, 170
- PLUM PIE (VEGAN), 171
- GOOSEBERRY PIE (VEGAN), 171
- BLUEBERRY PIE WITH AN OAT FLAKE CRUMBLE TOPPING (VEGAN), 172
- RHUBARB PIE (VEGAN), 175
- FOREST FRUIT PIE (VEGAN), 176
- APRICOT PIE (VEGAN), 179
- PANANE PIE, 180

WAFFLE FEST, 185

- HEART-SHAPED WAFFLES, 186
- MINI VANILLA OR CHOCOLATE BUTTER WAFFLES, 192
- CHOCOLATE-DIPPED LIÈGE WAFFLES, 195
- FLUFFY WAFFLES FOR STORING, 196

IN THE BISCUIT TIN, 199

- LONG BUTTER SHORTBREAD BISCUITS (BOTERTONGEN), 200
- COCONUT MACARONS, 203
- ALMOND HEARTS, 204
- CHERRY MARGUERITE, 205
- FLEMISH SPECULOOS, 207
- SPECULOOS BISCUITS (VEGAN), 207
- SMALL SHORTBREAD COOKIES (VEGAN), 208
- SWEET AND CRISPY BISCUITS, 209
- ACORNS, 210
- RICCIARELLI, 212
- MARQUISETTES, 213
- BELGIAN TRUFFLES, 214
- VANILLA PAIN À LA GRECQUE, 217

A CAKE FIT FOR A KING, 219

- LEMON BUNDT CAKE WITH LEMON FROSTING, 220
- POPPY SEED AND WHITE CHOCOLATE GANACHE BUNDT CAKE, 222
- PECAN AND MILK CHOCOLATE GANACHE BUNDT CAKE, 224
- BANANA AND WALNUT BUNDT CAKE, 227
- RASPBERRY AND CRUMBLE BUNDT CAKE, 228
- MILK CHOCOLATE AND SPECULOOS CRUMBLE MARBLE BUNDT CAKE, 230
- CHOCOLATE BUNDT CAKE, 232
- ALMOND BUNDT CAKE, 235

REGAL CAKES, 237

- PEAR AND BRÉSILIENNE CAKE ROYALE, 238
- APPLE AND STREUSEL CAKE ROYALE, 240
- APRICOT CAKE ROYALE, 241
- BLACKBERRY CAKE ROYALE, 242
- FIG AND CRUMBLE CAKE ROYALE, 244
- RASPBERRY CAKE ROYALE, 245
- REDCURRANT CAKE ROYALE, 246
- FOREST FRUIT CAKE ROYALE, 246

DELICIOUS SAVOURY BAKES, 249

- SAVOURY FLATBREAD, 250
- PIZZA TARTELETTE, 256
- CHAUSSON, 262
- BRIOCHE PISSALADIÈRE, 265
- GARNISHED QUICHE (QUICHE GARNIE), 266

FOREWORD

STEFAN ELIAS

"BAKING BRINGS HAPPINESS, MAKING PEOPLE HAPPY AND MAKING YOURSELF HAPPY."

In this book, I mainly elaborate on the recipes from *Het Belgisch Bakboek*, which I published in 2016. I searched for variations on these baking recipes with fruit, spices or toppings, exploring the incredible and infinite wealth of flavours you can add. On Instagram, I was introduced to the tasty treats of bakers from faraway places, from which I still draw a lot of inspiration. And on my travels, people gave me recipes that I recreated upon my return. You'll find, like I did, that what may look exotic and complicated is sometimes surprisingly simple and that it can be made with many of the staples that most people have in their pantry.

Baking brings happiness. The satisfaction of taking something out of the oven that you baked from scratch or savouring the taste of your homemade bread. The joy of being able to put something on the table that makes people visibly happy. Because baking makes people happy and it makes you happy. Tucking into pastries on a sunny Sunday morning, tearing and sharing a delicious savoury loaf of bread during a picnic with friends, cutting into a birthday cake, comforting a loved one with a cup of tea and a fragrant piece of cake.

But baking is also hard work. For beginners whose first attempt failed because they didn't knead their dough long enough or didn't use the exact ingredient weights. Baking takes time, dedication, precision and patience. It requires you to take it slow in a society obsessed with moving at a fast pace. For me, baking has also often been hard. At Bloch, the bakery in Ghent where I mastered this craft. The best possible place to learn but also the most demanding. Because my *patron*, Mr Bloch, may not have been the easiest person to work with. He insisted that we sell everything that other bakers had. Not a selection, mind. Everything. And if a customer asked for something we didn't have, he would invariably reply: "We don't have it today, but we will tomorrow."

It is hard graft, but I also have a lot of fun, like with the videos I make on YouTube to go with my cookbooks. People keep asking for more. Because baking provides warmth and cosiness, a sense of focus, allowing you to create something delicious and comforting with surprisingly simple ingredients. Over the years, interest has grown exponentially. I also notice this in the workshops I give: people often arrive feeling slightly uncertain, only to step out a few hours later with a bag full of delicious treats. Amazed at everything they made themselves in just a few hours and at how the afternoon flew by.

This is my fourth cookbook after *Het Belgisch Bakboek*, *Het Wereld Bakboek*, and *Het Feestbakboek*. I have written these books for you to introduce you to the wonderful world of baking, which is a feast in itself before the actual feast begins. To give you a taste of an unparalleled world of flavours with endless variations. To share tips and tricks, and inspire you to unleash your culinary creativity. But I also write these books for myself. They are my catalogue, my archive of recipes that I cannot and will not forget. These are delicacies that I enjoy. And rather than keeping them for myself, I prefer to share them with everyone.

I hope you will share them with your friends, family and loved ones. Or enjoy them on your own, which is also fine. Have fun with them, and enjoy!

PATISSERIE BLOCH: A FAMILY BAKERY IN EVERY SENSE OF THE WORD

Bloch prides itself on a rich history. The bakery was founded in 1899 in the heart of the Belgian city of Ghent, in the Veldstraat, by the Bloch family, who wanted to share their passion for bread and pastries. Locals soon found their way to the Boulangerie Viennoise, as it was known in those days.

In the early years, Bloch mainly specialised in traditional Ghent specialities, such as the famous Ghent bread and various types of pastries. The recipes were carefully preserved and passed down from generation to generation. Over time, the bakery was renamed Patisserie Alsacienne, a reference to the Bloch family's origins.

In the 1960s and 1970s, the bakery, with Jacques Bloch at its helm, expanded its range of innovative products to include various types of artisan breads, pastries and patisserie. Flavours from different worlds were included in the already extensive range.

The 1980s and 1990s proved somewhat challenging, with the rise of industrial bakeries and changes in the food industry. But Bloch always remained true to its artisan tradition, its emphasis on quality and its unrivalled customer service. The bakery thus managed to maintain and even strengthen its position in Ghent and beyond.

Bloch closed its doors in 2008, but the story did not end there. In 2015, two entrepreneurs from East Flanders decided to breathe new life into the bakery, together with Stefan Elias, former chef at the bakery. Their intention was to share all the unique products and recipes with the public again. In 2020, the bakery reopened on Sint-Pietersnieuwstraat in Ghent.

Today, Bloch is the go-to for freshly baked bread, pastries and many other sweets, as well as an important pillar of the community in Ghent, a city where this establishment earns a special place thanks to the emphasis it places on tradition and heritage as well as on innovation and enterprise.

INTRODUCTION

GREET DRAYE

(Centre for Agrarian History Leuven, Belgium)

Grain always plays a starring role in baking, whether you are making something savoury or sweet, a bread, cake or pie. The path from grain to bread and other pastries has been a long one. But every step along the way helped shape the subsequent culinary history of regions, countries and continents. So does the collection of recipes in this *Home Baking Book*. Moreover, given the ever smaller world we live in, it is a remarkably diverse collection. Ingredients and recipes travelled – and continue to travel – ever further, much like people. Building bridges between all kinds of places. So this book is a reflection of the world we live in. Belgian pastries are no longer limited to treats of Belgian origin. These days, they include all pastries made in Belgium.

Baking originated as home baking, and as such, it has been a part of our lives since time immemorial. It did, however, fade into the background very gradually throughout the centuries. Buying bread and pastries from local bakers became increasingly easier and cheaper, especially from the nineteenth century onwards. These days, home baking is all the rage again: people crave 'good bread', made with good ingredients, that has been baked slowly, 'like the good old days'. This desire has, in turn, encouraged a generation of professional bakers to change tack, and it has inspired historians to find out how people used to do things here and elsewhere, and to delve deeper into the role of bread and pastries. Bread, its makers and eaters, the craft of baking, the many traditions associated with it, and its social functions: this is all part of bread culture. Bread culture is very much a thing in many places around the world.

FROM WHEAT TO FLATBREAD

Grain is a collective name for the seeds of grasses. About 12,000 years ago, cereals were domesticated almost simultaneously in three places around the world: in China, the Middle East and Central America. From there, cereal cultivation spread to the rest of the world. Before this, humans also collected and ate wild grains, but in small amounts. By cultivating these species – i.e. deliberately sowing them – yields increased, and cereals became the most important staple of the human diet for a very long time. Different species were grown in various regions. In Europe, people mainly thrived on barley, wheat, rye and spelt. In Asia, rice thrived best, whereas maize was the main crop in Central and South America. In North America, maize and later also wheat were grown, whereas Africa relied on millet and sorghum.

Raw cereal grains had very little flavour, were difficult to digest, and had limited nutritional value. Roasted grains, on the other hand, were tastier and more nutritious, and they could be kept longer. Grains only became truly nutritious when they were threshed, ground and cooked into gruel. Grain grinding was first done manually, between two stones or with a stick in a log or bowl. You could cook a gruel from any kind of grain. These days, you can still find cereal gruel all over the world, from polenta over porridge to oatmeal and maize *putu pap*.

Over time, people continued to experiment with this mixture of cooked grains. It could be dried on a stone or baked into a cake. The gruel – the dough – did not rise, so the baked cake was flat. In that sense, it was not yet a real bread but a flour cake or flatbread. In 2018, some crumbs of flatbread were recovered from a fire pit at an archaeological site in northern Jordan, dating back to this period of cereal domestication. The technique of baking flatbread spread to the rest of the world. Like porridge, flatbread could be made from just about any grain. Other benefits included the fact that flatbread was easy to carry and could serve as a plate for other food items. Contemporary versions of flatbread can be found on every continent. They include pizza, *tarte flambée*, pita, crispbread (knäckebröd), focaccia, naan, papadum, matse, tortilla, roti, *bannock* and *injera*.

RISEN BREAD

The Egyptians are credited with discovering – by accident – that dough could rise. Around 1500 BC, some leftover dough was added to a new dough to avoid losing it. The wild yeast spores in the air and lactic acid bacteria had done their job in this forgotten bread, leading to spontaneous fermentation. The bread that was baked with the mixed dough was appreciated for its lightness. From that point onwards, people baked both fermented and unfermented bread. Besides ordinary bread, Egyptians also baked party breads. These breads were sweetened with honey, figs and dates, and offered to the gods.

From Egypt, bread-baking techniques spread to the rest of the Mediterranean and were perfected over time. The Greeks, for example, designed closed ovens. Around the second century BC, the Romans also discovered sourdough bread. They developed ingenious mechanical mills that could grind much finer grain, and by the first century CE, Rome had as many as three hundred professional bakers. Unlike flatbread, you could not bake risen bread from all grains back then. The Romans mainly stuck to wheat and barley, using oil and lard, as well as cumin, pepper, caraway, fennel, sesame and poppy seeds to enrich the flavour of their bread. Besides their savoury breads, they baked sweet breads with butter, milk, eggs, honey and fruit. In time, they also used rye, oats and spelt to bake risen bread.

Roman baking techniques and their favourite grains soon found their way to even the furthest outposts of the vast Roman Empire, from North Africa across Asia Minor to north-western Europe, including parts of what is known as the United Kingdom today, where they blended with local customs and crops. Professional bakers themselves, however, did not spread far and wide, only cropping up in the late Middle Ages. In those parts of Africa that were not exposed to Roman influences, in Asia and the Americas, people initially did not bake much risen bread: the grains that were grown there at the time were not suited for this. Not much has changed since then, especially in Asia and Africa. Flatbread and gruel continue to be the main cereal products in large parts of the world. However, both risen and unrisen bread gradually became more important across all these continents. It played a significant role in various religions and became part of social interactions. As early as the first century CE, the Roman poet Juvenalis knew that politicians could win the hearts of people with bread and games.

Before the advent of (many) professional bakeries, everyone, anywhere in the world, was a home baker. Or, more accurately, everyone baked their own bread. Baking was easy to do at home: on a griddle or in a pan over an open fire. Usually, however, baking was done in a communal baking oven in a central location in the village or town. The shape of the ovens varied depending on the bread that people baked. Flatbread was light and thin, and only needed to be baked for a very short time. Flatbread ovens had an opening at the top. The flatbreads were 'glued' to the walls or placed on small layered baking trays. Ovens for risen and, therefore, heavier bread had an opening in the front and looked like small houses. The loaves were baked on the bottom of the oven. These ovens had to be piping hot, as this bread needed much longer to bake than flatbread. Looking after the fire, including gathering wood, was traditionally a woman's job in most places around the world.

RICH AND POOR

Unlike in southern Europe, people in north-western Europe would have to wait until the late Middle Ages for bread to replace gruel in their diet. This was most visible in the fields. In the early Middle Ages, people mainly grew gruel cereals such as oats and barley. By the late Middle Ages, wheat and rye had taken their place. There were, of course, regional differences: in the north of England, oats remained the main crop because of the wet climate, whereas in the south people mainly grew wheat. Rye was popular in Germany, whereas in France wheat was preferred. The conversion also became visible in the infrastructure: large granaries, grain mills, grain markets, more and more baking ovens on rural farms, and bakeries in cities.

By the end of the Middle Ages, the area where bread grains were grown and bread was baked also expanded. According to tradition, Christopher Columbus carried a sourdough starter with him when

he set foot on Caribbean soil in 1492, thus introducing bread to the Americas. This is difficult to ascertain with certainty. We do know for sure, however, that wheat cultivation was introduced to North America as part of the Columbian Exchange – the great exchange of plants, animals and diseases – that resulted from Columbus's journey and all subsequent voyages between Europe, Africa, the Americas and Asia. During the seventeenth century, in particular, wheat cultivation grew with leaps and bounds on the east coast of North America. And this wheat was also used to bake bread.

Conversely, maize and cane sugar found their way to Europe from the Americas. The cane sugar was produced by African enslaved people on American plantations. It arrived unrefined in European ports, where it was refined, making it an ideal ingredient for sweet pastries. From the sixteenth century onwards, but especially from the seventeenth century, handwritten or printed cookbooks included recipes for sweet pastries such as cakes or biscuits with sugar, in addition to recipes for roasts, stews and pies.

For many centuries, pies resembled bread, as the dough was quite similar. During the seventeenth century, however, pies gradually became lighter, as cooks recommended that egg whites be beaten. These cakes were not for everyone. Only the very rich, the nobility and royal families, could afford expensive overseas ingredients that added a twist to these cakes and pastries. Other ingredients besides sugar included rum, chocolate and exotic fruits. Cake and pastries were specifically baked to celebrate an occasion. Incidentally, in those days only the very rich could afford cookbooks and literate cooks who could read the recipes in those books. Cookbook authors looked across borders, borrowing recipes from their counterparts. Italian and French recipes thus found their way to the Low Countries, recipes from the Southern Netherlands travelled to the North, ingredients from Eastern Europe and the Ottoman Empire made it to the West, and vice versa. Variations of some types of pastries, such as *speculoos* and gingerbread, could be found all over Europe. There are no traces of a similar 'royal' sweet baking culture in Africa and distant Asia.

Cookbooks did not feature bread recipes. Baking bread was considered a mundane activity. The recipes were supposed to be known. It is worth noting, however, that in addition to cakes and pastries, bread was also a social marker. Wherever bread was eaten, there always was bread for the rich and bread for the poor. Poor people ate brown bread. Only the very rich ate bread made from pure wheat – white bread – on weekdays. Making white flour took time, which made it an expensive process. Ordinary people thus only ate this bread on festive occasions. Other festive 'pastries for the poor' included pancakes and waffles.

Baking bread may have seemed like a mundane activity, but it was of vital importance. Until the mid-eighteenth century, bread accounted for a substantial share of people's diet in the Western world, especially if you were poor. It is estimated that a working adult in the Low Countries would have consumed one kilo of bread per day, spread over four meals, accounting for three-quarters of the household budget. In years of poor grain harvests, high bread prices led to hunger and riots. There was even a Boston bread riot in the United States in the early eighteenth century. In 1766, increased bread prices caused considerable social unrest in Britain. In France, a *guerre des farines* (flour war) erupted in the spring of 1775. Governments tried to control these revolts with fixed grain prices and export restrictions. But sometimes, the government also had a hand in the riots. In Novgorod, Russia, riots broke out in 1650 because the government had sold large amounts of Russian grain to Sweden, causing the price of grain to rise very sharply very suddenly.

In other parts of the world, especially Africa and Asia, people continued to eat flatbread for the most part, but they were less dependent on it because they had access to alternatives. Tubers such as cassava and yam were important in Africa, while rice played a similar role in Asia. In Europe, from the second half of the eighteenth century, potato consumption provided an alternative to bread. Improved farming techniques also increased grain yields, and this was necessary: although people were consuming less bread per capita on average, the population was rising sharply, so more bread was needed in absolute terms.

MODERN TIMES

The nineteenth century was a century of great change: the emergence of nation-states, further colonisation, the industrial revolution and its socio-economic consequences… Although these developments unfolded on a macro-level, they were not without impact on the micro-level of bread and pastries. The new nation-states established themselves with institutions and constitutions, but as the century progressed, they also appropriated certain dishes as well as bread and cakes. And the older states did so too. Certain types of bread or pastries then became 'typically' British, French, German, Belgian, American… Or they were assigned a place name to claim their origin. The further expansion of colonies also created even more exchange than before. Popular ingredients from the colonies were brought back to the fatherland and vice versa. But in 1806, Napoleon, emperor of France, issued the Continental Blockade: British ships carrying products from British colonies were no longer allowed to dock in French ports. This meant nobody could get any cane sugar. Instead, Napoleon ordered that sugar beets be grown in his empire, which included later Belgium. Although this obligation was not initially successful, it did fuel the cultivation of sugar beets. And because it was produced locally, beet sugar was cheaper than cane sugar, which made sweet pastries slightly less exclusive.

Thanks to the Industrial Revolution, bakers also had access to better ovens with temperature control. This, in turn, improved the quality of bread and cakes. The scientific revolution that took place alongside the industrial one provided bakers with fresh and dry yeast – Fleischmann in the US, for example – but also sodium bicarbonate. Unlike yeast, it was odourless and tasteless, which made it ideal for the rising of finer pastries. Dr. Oetker helped disseminate baking powder, a combination of sodium bicarbonate and a powdered acid for even better baking results.

The Industrial Revolution also heralded the breakthrough of the bourgeoisie, who followed the example of the nobility in every way. Cookbooks that had long been reserved for the upper classes were now available in editions for middle-class ladies and their maids. They could prepare their own delicious pastries in their gas cookers at home. Or they could buy them. The second half of the nineteenth century saw not only ordinary bakeries for bread appearing on the streets of many European cities but also pastry shops that sold cakes, pastries and biscuits to accompany coffee. The working class was a second social 'product' of the industrial revolution. Suddenly, many more people spent long days working outside their homes in factories, taking their lunch bread with them in a knapsack. The working class still ate a lot of brown bread. In many cases, though, they no longer baked this themselves. Home baking declined after 1850, not only in the cities but also in rural areas. Workers now bought their bread from (cooperative) bakeries or bread factories. Sometimes, the quality of this bread was substandard. Throughout the nineteenth century, complaints about bread that had been tampered with were manifold in the United States, Britain and continental Europe. For example, lime was added to increase the weight and hence the price. Bread prices continued to be a thorny issue for the working class. Massive European crop failures of both potatoes and cereals in the mid nineteenth century caused widespread famine.

The Industrial Revolution had a significant impact on bread and pastry culture, but it only took place in a small part of the world. Not much changed elsewhere. This would only happen in the twentieth century, following industrialisation. Or not at all, like in regions that to this day have not or hardly been industrialised. In the already industrialised world, however, some of the nineteenth-century trends continued into the twentieth century. Thus, just like earlier the bourgeoisie had discovered pastries through the nobility, in the twentieth century it was ordinary people who gradually, and especially after 1950, added them to their menu: at parties and for dessert. This can be explained by the fall in the price of sugar in the early twentieth century and by the fact that people's purchasing power was on the rise. Pastries could now be bought from bakeries, although they were also something people could bake at home. Cookbooks for rural and working-class women helped, as did the message that baking was fun and kept men home from the pub. Still, bread baking at home declined even further, after World War II even at a rapid pace. Bread consumption declined further, and after 1950, it was no longer deemed a vital ingredient.

After World War II, all kinds of migration boosted the exchange of bread and cakes that had always taken place. The world became much smaller. The important thing was no longer recipes or imported ingredients. With the migrants came the actual products in supermarkets, bakeries and restaurants. The growth of international tourism from the 1980s onwards broadened the world of bread and pastries even further.

INTANGIBLE CULTURAL HERITAGE

Something changed at the end of the twentieth century, however. In the midst of the globalised world's continuous exchange, complaints and concerns appeared in several places. Large-scale industrial production of bread and declining bread consumption posed a threat to artisan baking. At the same time, consumers also complained about the quality of (industrially produced) bread and pastries. Interestingly enough, this discontent did not lead people straight to their local baker. Rather, some resorted to baking bread and sweets themselves again. In doing so, they reverted to the old recipes and the traditions of 'the good old days'. By this they understood: starting from old, local grains that had not been processed very much, working with sourdough instead of yeast, kneading, and baking bread themselves in artisanal, wood-fired ovens. Some professional bakers also chose the same path. This inspired a sense of pride in mastering centuries-old crafts and reviving local or national traditions. Because this was also a factor: people feared that not only quality was at risk of being lost but also something that belonged to a specific place and community.

People gradually came to realise that bread and also pastries were *and are* heritage: not movable or immovable heritage, but intangible heritage. The kind of heritage that cannot be kept in a museum or archive. Intangible heritage requires safeguarding: people continuing the craft and its social or cultural traditions, and passing them on to future generations. The Representative List of the World's Intangible Cultural Heritage, compiled by UNESCO in 2003, lists several bread and baking traditions from around the world. The French baguette is arguably the best-known bread in Europe and the United States. Also on the list are Maltese *il-ftira* bread, Armenian lavash, several Central Asian flatbread traditions and Croatian gingerbread. Today, baking traditions are cherished all around the world, even if they are not on this list. This book provides a valuable contribution to this end.

BIBLIOGRAPHY

H. Eiselen, Brotkultur (Cologne, 1995).

S. Kaplan, *Good Bread Is Back. A Contemporary History of French Bread, the Way It Is Made, and the People Who Make It* (Durham – London 2006).

A. Pasqualone, 'Traditional Flatbreads Spread from the Fertile Crescent: Production Process and History of Baking Systems', in: *Journal of Ethnic Foods*, 5 (2018), pp. 10-19.

P. Scholliers, *Brood. Een geschiedenis van bakkers en hun brood* (Antwerp 2021).

R. Ysewijn, *Oats in the North, Wheat from the South. The History of British Baking: Savoury and Sweet* (Sydney – London 2020).

THE GOLDEN RULES OF BAKING

YEAST

All the recipes in this book use fresh yeast. Use half the quantity of fresh yeast stated in the recipe if you are using instant powdered yeast. If you are using liquid yeast, add 50% more yeast.

DOUGH

Whether on a scale or in cups, teaspoons or tablespoons, always weigh all the ingredients first. The liquids too! A litre of milk weighs more than a litre of water.

I prefer to weigh with a scale. Using cups, teaspoons or tablespoons will always result in some deviation from the recipe, even if very small. This matters because in baking and patisserie, weighing everything with precision is essential for obtaining optimal results.

Make sure the flour is not too cold. Unless the recipe specifically calls for cold ingredients, all your baking ingredients should be at room temperature.

Put the ingredients in a bowl as indicated, and stir with one hand (holding the bowl with your other hand) until everything is combined. Scrape the dough out onto your work surface, and knead it firmly with both hands, constantly pushing the dough away from you with the heel of your palm, working it until smooth. This can sometimes take up to 10 minutes.

KNEADING

Kneading serves a few functions. You mix the ingredients evenly, causing the protein molecules to form a gluten network and ensuring strength and elasticity. Dough temperature matters and is needed for the dough to rise. The warmer the dough, the faster it will rise, and the result will be less appetising. Dough that is too cold will come out sticky and rise too slowly. The optimum temperature for most doughs is around 25°C (50°F).

You can knead the bread dough by hand or use a stand mixer (e.g. KitchenAid or Kenwood). Always follow the recipe. Do not add liquid or flour, even if you think you should. A recipe is a recipe.

When using a stand mixer, knead bread slowly for at least 10 minutes. The quicker you knead, the hotter the dough gets, which impacts its function and flavour. Do the windowpane test to see if your dough is fully kneaded. Gently stretch a small portion of the dough. If properly kneaded, it will be elastic and form a membrane through which you can see light. If it breaks while stretching, you will need to knead it longer. When the dough is fully kneaded, shape it into a ball, and let it rise according to the recipe.

PROOFING/RESTING YOUR DOUGH (FIRST RISE AND SECOND RISE)

Make sure the dough is always covered with cling film or a clean cloth during rising to prevent it from forming a crust prematurely.

The dough develops its flavour during proofing (alcohol and sugars are formed). The first rise can take anything from 5 minutes to an hour. After the first rise, degas your dough using the slap-and-fold method. Degassing strengthens the gluten network, improving the loaf's volume.

The second rise can range from 0 to 20 minutes. During this stage, fermentation resumes. After the second rise, degas the dough again, shape it into a loaf, and let the dough rise for another hour or slightly longer. This is the final rise. Then bake it at the right temperature. Ambient temperature is very important for proofing. Make sure the work area is not cold and the dough is always covered with a cloth or cling film.

(OB)LONG LOAVES

Lightly dust your work surface with flour. Flip the dough over with the tucked ends facing up, and push it out as flat as you can. Fold the dough from bottom to top to form a crescent shape. Press firmly. Fold the left and right sides towards the middle, and press the dough firmly again. Roll the dough down in three iterations using your fingers. Press the seam to seal with your fingers, and roll the dough out to the desired length.

ROUND LOAVES

Lightly dust your work surface with flour. Flip the dough over with the tucked ends facing up, and use your hands to drag the dough and form a round. Fold the bottom of the circle up to the middle, and press it down with the tips of your fingers. Continue to fold the other sides until you have a uniform, taut ball. Flip the dough over, and transfer it to the baking tray with the seam facing down. Press the dough slightly.

SANDWICH ROLLS

Press the ball of dough flat to form a round. Roll the dough down in three iterations using your fingers. Press the seam to seal with your fingers. Place both your hands on top of the sandwich rolls and roll by moving both your hands outward to form tapered ends. If necessary, lightly dust your work surface with flour when rolling out the dough. Rubbing on excess flour as you knead can result in unwanted raw flour mixing into your dough, increasing the chances of your dough becoming dry and crumbly. Use baking paper to roll out sticky dough. The dough is easier to remove on baking paper. Brush with egg wash to provide a rich golden brown, shiny finish. Beat an egg and use a brush to spread it evenly.

ADDING STEAM

Add steam to your oven for rolls with an extra-crispy, shiny crust. The steam condenses, preventing the crust from forming too soon (because the dough surface is cooler than the steam). The bread's texture will be more even. Some tips for incorporating steam into your baking:

- While preheating your oven, place a baking tray on the bottom rack of the oven. As you slide your rolls into the oven, pour some water into the tray or throw in some ice cubes, and then quickly close the oven door.
- You can also spray water on the oven floor and wall with a spray bottle after you have put your bread into the oven. Then quickly close the oven.

BAKING

Respect the rising and baking times. These are necessary for a crispy crust and a nice flavour.

Preheat your oven to the specified temperature. While this is usually mentioned in step 1 of the recipes, it is best done about 15 minutes before you use the oven. **All the recipes in this book are baked in a conventional oven.** This is a standard oven with electrical heating elements at the top and/or bottom which deliver heat inside the oven cavity. For convection or fan ovens, I recommend setting your oven temperature to 20°C (40°F) cooler than indicated. Gas ovens have gas mark numbers. Gas mark 3 is 180°C (350°F), and gas mark 5 is 220°C (425°F). Check regularly during baking to avoid surprises. Always use a timer.

Remove bread from the tin immediately after it's baked and place it on a wire rack. Otherwise, it will go 'sweaty', loses its crispness, and will also dry out sooner. Damp bakeware also tends to rust..

BLIND BAKING

Blind baking is the process of baking a pie crust without the filling. Line the mould with the dough and prick holes into the dough with a fork (docking) to prevent it from puffing up. Line the dough with baking paper and then weigh it down with special pie weights or dry beans.

WEIGHTS AND MEASURES

Quantity	In ml
1 teaspoon	5 ml
1 tablespoon	15 ml
1 glass	250 ml
1 cup	250 ml
1 cup water	240 ml
1 cup milk	250 ml
1 cup flour	125 ml

Quantity	In g
1 teaspoon	5 to 10 g (0.18 to 0.35 oz)
1 tablespoon	15 to 20 g (0.53 to 0.71 oz)
1 pinch	the amount you can hold between your thumb and index finger
three-finger pinch	about 3 pinches
1 egg	50 to 60 g (1.76 to 2.1 oz)

PASTRY BASICS

APRICOT JAM
MAKES ABOUT 500 G (17.6 OZ)

- 300 G (1 ¼ CUPS, 10.6 OZ) APRICOT PUREE WITHOUT CHUNKS
- 200 G (1 CUP, 7.1 OZ) CASTER SUGAR
- SOME WATER TO LIQUEFY THE JAM

1. Add the sugar to the apricot puree, and stir to obtain jam.
2. Blend well with a hand blender. Add some water if the jam is too thick to spread on pastries or cakes.

Tip: You can also buy apricot jam in shops. Reduce with some water until it thickens for use on pastries.

APRICOT JAM FOR DECORATING
MAKES ABOUT 100 G (3.5 OZ)

- 75 G (½ CUP, 2.7 OZ) APRICOT JAM
- 25 G (3 TBSP, 0.8 OZ) WATER

1. Boil the jam with the water in a saucepan.
2. Use it immediately.

ALMOND CREAM (FRANGIPANE)
MAKES ABOUT 225 G (8 OZ)

- 50 G (4 TBSP, 1.76 OZ) UNSALTED BUTTER, ROOM TEMPERATURE
- 50 G (⅔ CUP, 1.76 OZ) FINELY GROUND ALMONDS
- 50 G (⅓ CUP, 1.76 OZ) ICING SUGAR
- 1 EGG
- 20 G (2 TBSP, 0.71 OZ) ALL-PURPOSE FLOUR
- A PINCH OF SALT

1. In a bowl, whisk butter until fluffy. Add the other ingredients, and stir vigorously with a spatula for 2 minutes.
2. Store in the refrigerator.

PASTRY CREAM (CRÈME PÂTISSIÈRE)
MAKES ABOUT 700 G (1 LB 8 OZ)

- 500 G (2 CUPS, 17.6 OZ) WHOLE MILK
- ½ VANILLA POD OR 10 G (1 TBSP, 0.35 OZ) VANILLA SUGAR
- 40 G (⅓ CUP, 1.41 OZ) CORNFLOUR
- 4 EGG YOLKS
- 125 G (⅔ CUP, 4.4 OZ) CASTER SUGAR

1. In a saucepan, bring the milk and the split vanilla pod or vanilla sugar to a boil.
2. In a bowl, mix the cornflour with the remaining milk with a whisk until smooth. Add the egg yolks and sugar, and whisk. Tip in some of the boiling milk, whisking well.
3. Tip the egg/milk mixture into the remaining boiling milk, and cook over low heat, whisking continuously until the cream thickens.

BASIC BRIOCHE DOUGH
MAKES ABOUT 500 G (17.6 OZ)

- 40 G (1.41 OZ) FRESH YEAST OR 1 ½ TBSP (0.49 OZ) INSTANT DRY YEAST
- 65 G (¼ CUP, 2.2 OZ) WHOLE MILK, COLD
- 1 EGG
- 260 G (2 CUPS, 9.2 OZ) BREAD FLOUR
- 20 G (2 TBSP, 0.71 OZ) GRANULATED SUGAR
- 75 G (5 TBSP, 2.7 OZ) UNSALTED BUTTER
- 5 G (1 TSP, 0.18 OZ) SALT

1. Put the yeast in a large bowl (if fresh yeast, crumble it), and combine with the cold milk and egg until smooth. Add flour, sugar, butter and salt, and continue mixing to form a homogeneous mass.
2. Pour out the dough on the work surface, and knead for 6 to 8 minutes until the dough appears very silky and elastic. Check with the windowpane test.
3. You will notice that the dough becomes quite sticky. Do not add flour but continue kneading until the dough no longer sticks to the work surface. It is important to scrape the dough often with a scraper and work in a room where it is not too hot.

PUFF PASTRY (FRENCH METHOD) (see pp. 30–31)
MAKES ABOUT 590 G (20 OZ)

- 250 G (1 CUP, 8.8 OZ) PLAIN FLOUR (HIGH PROTEIN CONTENT)
- 5 G (1 TSP, 0.18 OZ) SALT
- 60 G (4 TBSP, 2.1 OZ) UNSALTED BUTTER, ROOM TEMPERATURE
- 115 G (½ CUP, 0.40 OZ) ICE WATER
- 160 G (6 OZ) UNSALTED BUTTER FROM THE REFRIGERATOR

1. Work in a cold room. Mix the flour with the salt and the butter (2.1 oz). Add the ice water and knead briefly. Let rest for 10 minutes.
2. Roll out the dough and form a 1 cm (0.39 in) thick square. On a piece of baking paper, soften the cold butter with a rolling pin until 0.5 cm (0.20 in) thick. Cut into a square. Place the butter square in a diamond shape on the dough, and fold the dough corners over the butter. Make sure the butter is securely wrapped in the dough.
3. Give the dough six turns of three. Do this as follows. Roll out the entire assembly with a rolling pin until thin enough (8 to 10 mm (0.31 to 0.39 in)) to optimally distribute the fat. Take the bottom third of the dough, fold it over the middle third, then fold the top third over the middle third (this is the first of three turns). Rotate the dough 90 degrees, and repeat five more times. Let the dough rest in the refrigerator for 15 minutes between each rotation.

Tip: Making puff pastry is quite labour intensive. Alternatively, you can buy rolled-out puff pastry in the supermarket.

BUTTER CRUMBLE TOPPING
MAKES ABOUT 200 G (7 OZ)
- 50 G (4 TBSP, 1.76 OZ) UNSALTED BUTTER OR MARGARINE (VEGAN), ROOM TEMPERATURE
- 50 G (5 TBSP, 1.76 OZ) GRANULATED SUGAR
- 100 G (⅔ CUP, 3.5 OZ) ALL-PURPOSE FLOUR

1. In a bowl, whisk the butter until fluffy.
2. Using your hands, rub the sugar and flour into the butter with your fingertips. Don't knead!

BUTTER PASTRY OR LARD PASTRY
MAKES ABOUT 225 G (8 OZ)
- 100 G (⅔ CUP, 3.5 OZ) ALL-PURPOSE FLOUR
- 50 G (⅓ CUP, 1.76 OZ) ICING SUGAR
- A PINCH OF SALT
- 50 G (4 TBSP, 1.76 OZ) UNSALTED BUTTER, ROOM TEMPERATURE
- ½ EGG

1. Make the dough an hour in advance so it can stiffen properly.
2. Put all the ingredients in a bowl, and squeeze with your hands to form a homogeneous mass. Don't knead!
3. Wrap the dough in cling film, and proof it in the refrigerator.

Tip: You can store the dough for a long time in the freezer. Remember to wrap the dough in cling film.

BUTTERCREAM FROSTING
MAKES ABOUT 275 G (9.5 OZ)
- 1 EGG
- 30 G (3 TBSP, 1.06 OZ) WATER
- 100 G (½ CUP, 3.5 OZ) GRANULATED SUGAR
- 115 G (4 OZ) UNSALTED BUTTER, ROOM TEMPERATURE

1. Beat the egg.
2. Boil the water with the sugar until the mixture has reached 119°C (245°F). Add the sugar syrup to the beaten egg. Keep whisking until the mixture reaches room temperature.
3. Add the butter and continue whisking until you obtain buttercream frosting.

Tip: For a quick buttercream frosting, the ratio is ½ part softened butter to ½ part icing sugar. The taste will probably differ from the first version.

HAZELNUT *BRÉSILIENNE*
MAKES ABOUT 75 G (2.7 OZ)
- 45 G (4 TBSP, 1.59 OZ) GRANULATED SUGAR
- 15 G (3 TSP, 0.53 OZ) WATER
- 30 G (⅕ CUP, 1.06 OZ) PEELED HAZELNUTS, LIGHTLY ROASTED TO IMPART MORE FLAVOUR

1. Cook the sugar and water over medium-high heat until it caramelises. Do not stir the mixture. Remove from heat as soon as the sugar starts to darken. Fold in the hazelnuts with a spoon.
2. Line a cutting board with baking paper. Tip out the mixture (note: it is very hot) and leave to cool.
3. Finely chop into *brésilienne*.

BROYAGE
MAKES ABOUT 240 G (8.5 OZ)
- 120 G (¾ CUP, 4.2 OZ) FINELY GROUND ALMONDS
- 120 G (1 CUP, 4.2 OZ) ICING SUGAR

Mix the almond meal with the icing sugar to form a homogeneous mass.

CHOCOLATE CURLS

1. Spread tempered chocolate (see baking glossary, p. 33) into a thin layer over a cold marble or other clean surface. Let it solidify.
2. Lightly scrape a paring knife at an angle across the chocolate to make curls. You can also grate hard chocolate.

CHOCOLATE PASTE
MAKES ABOUT 200 G (7.1 OZ)
- 80 G (⅓ CUP, 2.8 OZ) CREAM (40% FAT)
- 100 G (⅔ CUP, 3.5 OZ) DARK CHOCOLATE, CHOPPED
- ⅓ EGG

1. In a saucepan, boil the cream. Remove from heat. Mix in the chocolate pieces, followed by the egg.
2. Let cool briefly to a spreadable consistency.

FONDANT SUGAR
MAKES ABOUT 200 G (7.1 OZ)
- 175 G (1½ CUP, 6.1 OZ) ICING SUGAR
- 25 G (3 TBSP, 0.8 OZ) WATER

Over low heat, dissolve the icing sugar in the water while stirring. This takes very little time. Make sure the sugar is never hotter than your body temperature. Check the temperature regularly with your finger. When the fondant sugar reaches body temperature, it will also appear shiny on your cake. If it gets too hot, it will appear dull, and the sugar will crumble after cooling.

Tip: Use a pastry brush to apply it to the cake. You can also dip the top of the cake in the fondant sugar, removing any excess with your fingertips.

FONDANT SUGAR WITH COCOA
MAKES ABOUT 200 G (7.1 OZ)
- 170 G (1½ CUP, 6 OZ) ICING SUGAR
- 5 G (1 TSP, 0.18 OZ) COCOA POWDER
- 25 G (3 TBSP, 0.8 OZ) WATER

Over low heat, dissolve the icing sugar in the water with the cocoa powder while stirring. This takes very little time. Make sure the sugar is never hotter than your body temperature. Check the temperature regularly with your finger. When the fondant sugar reaches body temperature, it will also appear shiny on your cake. If it gets too hot, it will appear dull, and the sugar will crumble after cooling.

Tip : Use a pastry brush to apply it to the cake. You can also dip the top of the cake in the fondant sugar, removing any excess with your fingertips.

GANACHE
MAKES ABOUT 200 G (7.1 OZ)
- 100 G (⅖ CUP, 3.5 OZ) CREAM (40% FAT)
- 100 G (⅔ CUP, 3.5 OZ) DARK CHOCOLATE, ROUGHLY CHOPPED

1. In a saucepan, boil the cream. Remove from heat. Mix in the chocolate pieces, and leave to cool to body temperature.
2. If the ganache is too cold and hard, you can warm it up while stirring until it becomes squirtable or liquid again.

RISEN PUFF PASTRY (see pp. 30–31)
MAKES 16 PASTRIES
- 60 G (2.1 OZ) FRESH YEAST OR 2 ½ TBSP (0.81 OZ) INSTANT DRY YEAST
- 280 G (1 ⅙ CUP, 9.9 OZ) WHOLE MILK, COLD
- 500 G (4 CUPS, 17.6 OZ) BREAD FLOUR
- 50 G (¼ CUP, 1.76 OZ) GRANULATED SUGAR
- 40 G (3 TBSP, 1.41 OZ) UNSALTED BUTTER, ROOM TEMPERATURE
- 10 G (2 TSP, 0.35 OZ) SALT
- 250 G (8.8 OZ) UNSALTED BUTTER FROM THE REFRIGERATOR

1. Work in a cold room. Dissolve the yeast in cold milk. Add the flour, sugar, salt and unsalted butter at room temperature, and mix to form a homogeneous mass. Knead the dough for a few minutes until it no longer sticks to the work surface. Do not add more flour while kneading.
2. Using a rolling pin, roll the dough into a 6 mm (¼ in) thick rectangle measuring 15 × 40 cm (6 × 15.75 in).
3. Soften the hard bakery butter by tapping it with the rolling pin and form a 15 × 25 cm (6 × 9.85 in) rectangle (place the butter between two sheets of baking paper). Cover two-thirds of the dough with the butter. Take the section that is not covered by the butter, and fold it over half of the buttered rectangle. Now fold the other side of the buttered rectangle over this. Press firmly.
4. Give the dough two turns of three. Do this as follows. Roll out the entire assembly to form a rectangle measuring 20 × 60 cm (7.87 × 23.61 in). Fold the left third of the dough over the middle third, then fold the right third over it. Now you have a dough with three layers (turn 1). Rotate the dough 90 degrees and repeat (turn 2).
5. Let the dough stiffen in the refrigerator for 30 minutes before working it further. If you notice during turns that the butter has become too soft, place the dough in the refrigerator for a short time.

ROASTED SLICED ALMONDS
- SLICED ALMONDS

1. Line a baking tray with baking paper. Preheat the oven to 200ºC (400ºF).
2. Spread the amount you need for the recipe you are making on the baking tray. Roast the almonds lightly in the oven at 200ºC (400ºF) for 7 to 10 minutes.

ROASTED HAZELNUTS
- PEELED HAZELNUTS

1. Line a baking tray with baking paper. Preheat the oven to 200ºC (400ºF).
2. Spread the amount you need for the recipe you are making on the baking tray. Roast the hazelnuts lightly in the oven at 200ºC (400ºF) for 7 to 10 minutes.

SALTED BRIOCHE DOUGH
MAKES ABOUT 400 G (14.1 OZ)
- 10 G (0.35 OZ) YEAST OR 1 TBSP (0.13 OZ) INSTANT DRY YEAST
- 60 G (¼ CUP, 2.1 OZ) WHOLE MILK
- 210 G (1 ¾ CUP, 7.4 OZ) BREAD FLOUR
- 1 EGG
- 5 G (1 TSP, 0.18 IN) SALT
- 60 G (4 TBSP, 2.1 OZ) UNSALTED BUTTER, ROOM TEMPERATURE

1. Dissolve the yeast in the milk. Mix in the flour, egg, salt and butter to form a homogeneous mass.
2. Knead on the work surface for 6 minutes until smooth and elastic.

OAT FLAKE CRUMBLE TOPPING
MAKES ABOUT 100 G (3.5 OZ)
- 25 G (2 TBSP, 0.88 OZ) UNSALTED BUTTER OR MARGARINE (VEGAN) AT ROOM TEMPERATURE
- 40 G (⅕ CUP, 1.55 OZ) GRANULATED SUGAR
- 35 G (⅓ CUP, 1.23 OZ) OAT FLAKES

1. In a bowl, whisk butter until fluffy.
2. Using your hands, rub the sugar and oat flakes into the butter with your fingertips. Don't knead!

HAZELNUT PASTE
MAKES ABOUT 225 G (0.8 OZ)
- 50 G (4 TBSP, 1.76 OZ) UNSALTED BUTTER, ROOM TEMPERATURE
- 50 G (⅖ CUP, 1.76 OZ) FINELY GROUND ROASTED HAZELNUTS
- 50 G (⅓ CUP, 1.76 OZ) ICING SUGAR
- 1 EGG
- 20 G (2 TBSP, 0.71 OZ) ALL-PURPOSE FLOUR
- A PINCH OF SALT

1. In a bowl, whisk butter until creamy, mix in the other ingredients, and stir vigorously for 2 minutes.
2. Store in the refrigerator.

CHEESE SAUCE
MAKES ABOUT 600 G (21 OZ)
- 350 G (1 ½ CUP, 12.3 OZ) WHOLE MILK
- 40 G (3 TBSP, 1.41 OZ) UNSALTED BUTTER
- 40 G (¼ CUP, 1.41 OZ) ALL-PURPOSE FLOUR
- 0.5 G (¼ TSP, 0.02 OZ) GROUND BLACK PEPPER
- 3 G (½ TSP, 0.11 OZ) SALT
- 1 EGG YOLK
- 125 G (1 ⅓ CUP, 4.3 OZ) EMMENTAL CHEESE
- 20 G (⅓ CUP, 0.71 OZ) GRATED CHEDDAR CHEESE

1. In a saucepan, bring the milk to the boil.
2. Melt the butter in another saucepan. Mix in the flour with a whisk to form a paste. Stir continuously as you cook it. This is the roux base.
3. Take both saucepans off the heat when the milk boils. Pour the boiling milk into the roux. Whisk until smooth. Stir to thicken over heat until you've reached the desired consistency.
4. Remove from heat and season with salt and pepper. Stir in another egg yolk and finally tip in the cheese.

MERINGUE COLD METHOD

MAKES ABOUT 225 G (0.80 OZ) OF MERINGUE

- 2.5 LARGE EGG WHITES
- 90 G (½ CUP, 3.2 OZ) GRANULATED SUGAR
- 60 G (½ CUP, 2.1 OZ) ICING SUGAR

1. In a bowl, whisk the egg whites until thick and foamy. Continue to whisk, and gradually add the granulated sugar spoon by spoon.
2. Do the same with the icing sugar, and whisk until the whites are smooth and glossy.

MERINGUE HOT METHOD (ITALIAN MERINGUE)

MAKES ABOUT 225 G (0.80 OZ) OF MERINGUE

- 50 G (⅕ CUP, 1.76 OZ) WATER
- 150 G (¾ CUP, 5.3 OZ) GRANULATED SUGAR
- 10 G (1 TBSP, 0.35 OZ) ICING SUGAR
- 2.5 LARGE EGG WHITES

1. Make a syrup by heating the water and the sugar in a saucepan with a heavy base. Use a cooking thermometer that goes to 150ºC (300ºF).
2. Once the temperature of the sugar syrup reaches 100ºC (210ºF), whisk the egg whites until they hold stiff peaks.
3. When the temperature of the syrup has reached 119ºC (245ºF), slowly pour the sugar syrup into the stiff egg whites, whisking continuously. Make sure not to pour the sugar syrup onto the whisk. Keep whisking until the whites are very smooth, glossy and stiff.

PECAN PASTE

MAKES ABOUT 225 G (0.80 OZ)

- 50 G (4 TBSP, 1.76 OZ) UNSALTED BUTTER, ROOM TEMPERATURE
- 50 G (⅖ CUP, 1.76 OZ) FINELY GROUND PECANS
- 50 G (⅓ CUP, 1.76 OZ) ICING SUGAR
- 1 EGG
- 20 G (2 TBSP, 0.71 OZ) ALL-PURPOSE FLOUR
- A PINCH OF SALT

1. In a bowl, whisk the butter until fluffy, mix in the other ingredients, and stir vigorously for 2 minutes.
2. Store in the refrigerator.

PESTO

- 135 G (5 CUPS, 4.8 OZ) BASIL LEAVES
- 45 G (⅓ CUP, 1.59 OZ) PINE NUTS
- 45 G (½ CUP, 1.59 OZ) GRATED PARMESAN CHEESE
- 25 G (3 TBSP, 0.88 OZ) OLIVE OIL
- 2 CLOVES OF GARLIC
- APPROX. 3 G (½ TSP, 0.11 OZ) SALT
- A PINCH OF WHITE PEPPER
- A FEW DROPS OF LEMON JUICE TO PRESERVE THE PESTO'S VIBRANT GREEN COLOUR

Mix all the ingredients and blend in a food processor or with a hand blender until smooth.

Tip: Make the pesto the day before so its flavour can develop.

PIZZA SAUCE

MAKES ABOUT 500 G (17.6 OZ)

- 300 G (10.6 OZ) CHICKEN OR VEGETABLE STOCK
- 8 G (1 TBSP, 0.28 OZ) SUGAR
- 2 G (1 TSP, 0.07 OZ) PROVENÇAL HERBS
- 22 G (½ BULB, 0.78 OZ) SHALLOTS
- 5 GARLIC CLOVES
- 30 G (2 TBSP, 1.06 OZ) BUTTER
- 16 G (2 TBSP, 0.56 OZ) OLIVE OIL
- PEPPER AND CAYENNE PEPPER TO TASTE
- 20 G (2 TBSP, 0.71 OZ) ALL-PURPOSE FLOUR
- 80 G (5 TBSP, 2.8 OZ) DOUBLE-CONCENTRATED TOMATO PUREE

1. Bring the stock, sugar and Provençal herbs to a boil.
2. Fry the shallots with the garlic in the butter and oil. Mix. Add pepper, cayenne pepper and flour. Stir over high heat until smooth.
3. Tip this mixture into the stock, and stir (over heat) until the sauce is completely smooth.
4. Turn off the heat, and stir the tomato puree into the sauce.
5. Add salt to taste if necessary.

HAZELNUT PRALINE PASTE

MAKES ABOUT 200 G (7.1 OZ)

- 125 G (1 CUP, 4.4 OZ) PEELED HAZELNUTS
- 25 G (3 TBSP, 0.8 OZ) WATER
- 75 G (⅖ CUP, 2.5 OZ) GRANULATED SUGAR
- 10 G (1 TBSP, 0.35 OZ) SUNFLOWER OIL

1. On a baking tray lined with baking paper, roast the hazelnuts for about 10 minutes in a 180ºC (350ºF) oven.
2. In a heavy-based saucepan, boil the water and sugar until a light caramel forms. Pour the caramel over the hazelnuts and leave to cool.
3. Break the mixture into pieces, and grind in a food processor with the oil to obtain a paste.

SUGAR SYRUP

MAKES ABOUT 200 G (7.1 OZ)

- 100 G (⅖ CUP 3.5 OZ) WATER
- 100 G (½ CUP, 3.5 OZ) GRANULATED SUGAR

In a saucepan, combine sugar and water. Bring to a boil, stirring until sugar has dissolved. Cool.

CHANTILLY CREAM

MAKES ABOUT 300 G (10.6 OZ)

- 260 G (1 CUP, 9.2 OZ) CREAM (35-40% FAT)
- 40 G (4 TBSP, 1.41 OZ) CASTER SUGAR

Whisk the cream and sugar vigorously to obtain Chantilly cream.

CHANTILLY CREAM WITH CHOCOLATE

MAKES ABOUT 310 G (1.09 OZ)

- 260 G (1 CUP, 9.2 OZ) CREAM (35-40% FAT)
- 40 G (4 TBSP, 1.41 OZ) CASTER SUGAR
- 10 G (2 TSP, 0.35 OZ) COCOA POWDER

1. Whisk the cream with the sugar until the cream is no longer liquid.
2. Add the sifted cocoa powder (sieving prevents clumping), and whisk until the cream is sufficiently firm.

CHOUX PASTRY (PÂTE À CHOUX)

MAKES ABOUT 400 G (14.1 OZ) OF CHOUX PASTRY

- 75 G WATER (⅓ CUP 2.7 OZ)
- 75 G WHOLE MILK (⅓ CUP, 2.7 OZ)
- 50 G (3 TBSP, 1.76 OZ) UNSALTED BUTTER
- A PINCH OF SALT
- 90 G (¾ CUP 3.2 OZ) BREAD FLOUR
- 160 G (3 LARGE EGGS, 5.6 OZ)

1. Heat the water, milk and butter with a pinch of salt, and bring to a boil.
2. Tip in the flour. Return to the heat and mix with a spatula until the dough is dry. Leave to cool for 10 minutes.
3. Mix in the eggs little by little (in 3 turns) to make a smooth, uniform dough.

STREUSEL
FOR 135 G (4.7 OZ)

- 20 G (1 TBSP, 0.71 OZ) UNSALTED BUTTER, ROOM TEMPERATURE
- 30 G (3 TBSP, 1.06 OZ) SHINY DECORATING SUGAR
- 50 G (¼ CUP, 1.76 OZ) GRANULATED SUGAR
- 1 G (½ TSP, 0.04 OZ) CINNAMON
- 20 G (⅛ CUP, 0.71 OZ) CHOPPED PEELED ALMONDS
- 15 G (1 TBSP, 0.53 OZ) ALL-PURPOSE FLOUR

1. In a bowl, whisk butter until fluffy.
2. Mix in the sugars, cinnamon and chopped almonds until you obtain a smooth mass.
3. Stir in the flour until the mixture becomes crumbly. Don't knead!

CAKE BASE AND FILLING PASTRY ROYALE
8 SERVINGS

- 100 G (7 TBSP, 3.5 OZ) UNSALTED BUTTER, ROOM TEMPERATURE
- 2 LARGE EGGS
- 100 G (½ CUP, 3.5 OZ) GRANULATED SUGAR
- 50 G (⅖ CUP, 1.76 OZ) FINELY GROUND PEELED ALMONDS
- 50 G (⅖ CUP, 1.76 OZ) FINELY GROUND ROASTED HAZELNUTS (SEE ABOVE)
- 1.5 G (⅓ TSP, 0.06 OZ) SALT
- 250 G (8.8 OZ) SHORTBREAD PASTRY (SEE PASTRY BASICS, P. 29)
- SOFT BUTTER FOR THE TART TRAY

1. Lightly grease a tart tray (10 × 36 cm (4 × 14.5 in), 2.5 cm (1 in) high) or a round tart tray (Ø 20 cm (7.87 in) and 2.5 cm (1 in) high) with butter. Use a tart tray with removable bottom. Preheat the oven to 180°C (350°F).
2. Put the butter in a bowl, and whisk until fluffy. Mix in the egg, granulated sugar, almond meal, hazelnut meal and salt, and stir vigorously with a spatula for 2 minutes.
3. Remove the dough from the refrigerator. Work it a little more with your hands. Roll it out with a rolling pin. Form a rectangle (14 × 38 cm (5.52 × 15 in)) or a round disc (Ø 23 cm (9.05 in)). Line the tart tray with the dough.
4. Prick the bottom of the pie crust and pour in the filling.

VLAAI PIE CRUST
FOR 1 CAKE OR 4 SERVINGS

- SOFT BUTTER FOR THE TART TRAY
- 10 G (0.35 OZ) FRESH YEAST OR 1 TBSP (0.13 OZ) INSTANT DRY YEAST
- 40 G (⅙ CUP, 1.41 OZ) WHOLE MILK
- 100 G (⅗ CUP, 3.5 OZ) BREAD FLOUR
- 10 G (1 TBSP, 0.5 OZ) GRANULATED SUGAR
- ½ TEASPOON SALT
- 40 G (3 TBSP, 1.41 OZ) UNSALTED BUTTER, ROOM TEMPERATURE
- 1 BEATEN EGG FOR AN EGG WASH

1. Grease a round 4-person tart tray (Ø 20 cm (7.87 in), 2.5 cm (1 in) high). Use a tart tray with removable bottom.
2. In a bowl, dissolve the yeast with the milk. Mix the flour with the sugar, salt and butter.
3. Pour out the dough on the work surface, and knead for 6 minutes until elastic. Shape into a ball and leave to rest for 15 minutes.
4. Roll out the dough into a Ø 23 cm (9.05 in) round disc and line the tart tray. Make sure you don't have any excess dough.
5. Press the dough gently into the form of the tin with your knuckles, and use your thumbs to push up the sides a little.
6. Brush the edge with the egg wash, and fill the tart with the filling of your choice.

PIE SAUCE
MAKES ABOUT 150 G

- 100 G (⅖ CUP, 3.5 OZ) WATER
- 10 G (3 TSP, 0.35 OZ) POTATO STARCH
- 50 G (¼ CUP, 1.76 OZ) GRANULATED SUGAR

1. Pour the water into a saucepan, and mix in the potato starch and sugar.
2. Put the saucepan on the hob, and let the sauce thicken while stirring. Use a whisk.
3. Remove the sauce from the heat once boiling.

VEGAN ALMOND PASTE
MAKES ABOUT 160 G (2.1 OZ)

- 40 G (3 TBSP, 1.41 OZ) GOOD-QUALITY MARGARINE
- 40 G (⅓ CUP, 1.41 OZ) FINELY GROUND ALMONDS
- 40 G (⅓ CUP, 1.41 OZ) ICING SUGAR
- 20 G (2 TBSP, 0.71 OZ) WATER
- 15 G (1 TBSP, 0.53 OZ) ALL-PURPOSE FLOUR
- A PINCH OF SALT

1. In a bowl, whisk margarine until fluffy, mix in the other ingredients, and stir vigorously for 2 minutes.
2. Store in the refrigerator.

VEGAN RISEN PUFF PASTRY (see pp. 30–31)
FOR 16 PASTRIES

- 60 G (2.1 OZ) FRESH YEAST OR 2 ½ TBSP (0.81 OZ) INSTANT DRY YEAST
- 250 G (1 CUP, 8.8 OZ) ALMOND MILK, COLD
- 500 G (4 CUPS, 17.6 OZ) BREAD FLOUR
- 50 G (¼ CUP, 1.76 OZ) GRANULATED SUGAR
- 40 G (3 TBSP, 1.41 OZ) GOOD-QUALITY MARGARINE, ROOM TEMPERATURE
- 10 G (2 TSP, 0.35 OZ) SALT
- 250 G (8.8 OZ) GOOD-QUALITY MARGARINE FROM THE REFRIGERATOR

1. Work in a cold room. Dissolve the yeast in the almond milk. Add the flour, the sugar, the salt and the room-temperature margarine, and mix to form a homogeneous mass. Knead the dough for a few minutes until it no longer sticks to the work surface. Do not add more flour while kneading.
2. Using a rolling pin, roll the dough into a 6 mm (¼ in) thick rectangle

measuring 15 × 40 cm (6 × 15.75 in).

3. Soften the hard margarine by tapping it with the rolling pin, and form a 15 × 25 cm (6 × 9.85 in) rectangle (place the butter between two sheets of baking paper). Cover two-thirds of the dough with the margarine. Take the section that is not covered by the margarine, and fold it over half of the rectangle with the margarine. Now fold the other side of the rectangle over this. Press firmly.
4. Give the dough two turns of three. Do this as follows. Roll out the entire assembly to form a rectangle measuring 20 × 60 cm (7.87 × 23.61 in). Fold the left third of the dough over the middle third, then fold the right third over it. Now you have a dough with three layers (turn 1). Rotate the dough 90 degrees and repeat (turn 2).
5. Let the dough stiffen in the refrigerator for 30 minutes before working it further. If you notice during turns that the margarine has become too soft, place the dough in the refrigerator for a short time.

VEGAN PECAN PASTE

FOR 160 G (2.1 OZ)

- 40 G (3 TBSP, 1.41 OZ) GOOD-QUALITY MARGARINE
- 40 G (⅓ CUP, 1.41 OZ) FINELY GROUND PECANS
- 40 G (⅓ CUP, 1.41 OZ) ICING SUGAR
- 20 G (2 TBSP, 0.71 OZ) WATER
- 15 G (1 TBSP, 0.53 OZ) ALL-PURPOSE FLOUR
- A PINCH OF SALT

1. In a bowl, whisk margarine until fluffy, mix in the other ingredients, and stir vigorously for 2 minutes.
2. Store in the refrigerator.

VEGAN *VLAAI* PIE CRUST

FOR 1 CAKE (4 SERVINGS)

- SOFT MARGARINE FOR THE TART TRAY
- 10 G (0.35 OZ) FRESH YEAST OR 1 TBSP (0.13 OZ) INSTANT DRY YEAST
- 40 G (⅙ CUP, 1.41 OZ) ALMOND MILK
- 100 G (⅘ CUP, 3.5 OZ) BREAD FLOUR
- 10 G (1 TBSP, 0.5 OZ) GRANULATED SUGAR
- ½ TEASPOON SALT
- 40 G (3 TBSP, 1.41 OZ) GOOD-QUALITY MARGARINE, ROOM TEMPERATURE

1. Grease a round 4-person tart tray (Ø 20 cm (7.87 in), 2.5 cm (1 in) high) with the soft margarine. Use a tart tray with removable bottom.
2. In a bowl, dissolve the yeast with the almond milk. Mix the flour with the sugar, salt and margarine.
3. Pour out the dough on the work surface, and knead for 6 minutes until smooth. Shape into a ball, and leave to rest for 15 minutes.
4. Roll out the dough into a Ø 23 cm (9.05 in) round disc, and line the cake tin. Make sure you don't have any excess dough.
5. Press the dough gently into the tart tray with your knuckles, and use your thumbs to push up the sides a little.
6. Brush the edge with some almond milk, and fill the tart with the filling of your choice.

VEGAN WALNUT PASTE

FOR 160 G (2.1 OZ)

- 40 G (3 TBSP, 1.41 OZ) GOOD-QUALITY MARGARINE
- 40 G (⅓ CUP, 1.41 OZ) FINELY GROUND WALNUTS
- 40 G (⅓ CUP, 1.41 OZ) ICING SUGAR
- 20 G (2 TBSP, 0.71 OZ) WATER
- 15 G (1 TBSP, 0.53 OZ) ALL-PURPOSE FLOUR
- A PINCH OF SALT

1. In a bowl, whisk margarine until fluffy, mix in the other ingredients, and stir vigorously for 2 minutes.
2. Store in the refrigerator.

MAKES ABOUT 225 G (8 OZ)

- 50 G (4 TBSP, 1.76 OZ) UNSALTED BUTTER, ROOM TEMPERATURE
- 50 G (⅖ CUP, 1.76 OZ) FINELY GROUND ALMONDS
- 50 G (⅓ CUP, 1.76 OZ) ICING SUGAR
- 1 EGG
- 20 G (2 TBSP, 0.71 OZ) ALL-PURPOSE FLOUR
- A PINCH OF SALT

WALNUT PASTE

FOR 225 G (8 OZ)

- 50 G (4 TBSP, 1.76 OZ) UNSALTED BUTTER
- 50 G (⅖ CUP, 1.76 OZ) FINELY GROUND WALNUTS
- 50 G (⅓ CUP, 1.76 OZ) ICING SUGAR
- 1 EGG
- 20 G (2 TBSP, 0.71 OZ) ALL-PURPOSE FLOUR
- A PINCH OF SALT

1. In a bowl, whisk butter until fluffy, mix in the other ingredients, and stir vigorously for 2 minutes.
2. Store in the refrigerator.

SHORTBREAD PASTRY (PÂTE SABLÉE)

FOR 400 G (15.5 OZ)

- 175 G (1 ⅓ CUP, 6 OZ) ALL-PURPOSE FLOUR
- 25 G (¼ CUP, 0.88 OZ) FINELY GROUND ALMONDS
- 65 G (½ CUP, 2.3 OZ) ICING SUGAR
- ¼ TEASPOON SALT
- 100 G (7 TBSP, 3.5 OZ) UNSALTED BUTTER, ROOM TEMPERATURE
- ¾ EGG

1. Make the dough an hour in advance so it can stiffen properly.
2. Put all the ingredients in a bowl, and squeeze with your hands to form a homogeneous mass. Don't knead.
3. Wrap the dough in cling film, and proof it in the refrigerator.

Tip: You can store the dough for a long time in the freezer. Remember to wrap the dough in cling film.

SELF-RISING FLOUR

MAKES ABOUT 1,035 G (37 OZ)

- 900 G (7 CUPS, 32 OZ) ALL-PURPOSE FLOUR
- 100 G (⅔ CUP, 3.5 OZ) CORNSTARCH
- 35 G (3 TBSP, 1.23 OZ) BAKING POWDER

Mix the flour with the cornstarch and baking powder, and sift.

SWISS CREAM (CRÈME SUISSE)

MAKES ABOUT 450 G (15.9 OZ)

- 325 G (12.5 OZ) PASTRY CREAM (SEE ABOVE)
- 125 G (½ CUP, 4.5 OZ) CHANTILLY CREAM (SEE ABOVE)

Combine the pastry cream with the Chantilly cream.

GLOSSARY

AU BAIN-MARIE

This is a cooking technique in which heat is applied to a container of water into which a second container of food is placed. The heat transfers slowly to the food, which eventually reaches the water's temperature. The advantage of this melting technique is that the food does not burn to the sides of the inner container.

- Milk chocolate (chopped): ½ cup (80 g, 2.82 oz) takes 4 minutes to melt.
- Dark chocolate (chopped): ½ cup (80 g, 2.82 oz) takes 4 minutes to melt.
- White chocolate (chopped): ½ cup (80 g, 2.82 oz) takes 3 minutes to melt.

BAKING POWDER

The baking powder which you buy in sachets from shops is generally a mixture of several baking powders (sodium bicarbonate, sodium pyrophosphate, and so on) with some starch.

BEATING EGG WHITES UNTIL STIFF

Use a clean grease-free bowl. Rinse your bowl with cold water, and dry it with kitchen paper. Make sure there are no traces of egg yolk in the egg whites. Add some sugar if the egg whites go grainy and flakes appear near the edge of the bowl. That way, the mixture will be smoother and less gritty.

BOILING MILK

Sometimes, the saucepan may burn when cooking milk. Avoid this by rinsing the pan with cold water. Pour in the milk and then cook it.

CREAMING BUTTER

This means softening the butter, not melting it.

DARK BROWN SUGAR

When available, use the dark variety of cassonade or kandijsuiker, a Belgian speciality made from sugar beet.

EGG YOLKS

Egg yolks clump when combined with sugar or salt. Always beat the yolks with the sugar or salt to form a homogeneous mass.

FOUR-SPICE POWDER

This spice blend contains grated nutmeg, ground cinnamon, cloves, and finely ground allspice (allspice is also called Jamaica pepper).

HEATING FONDANT SUGAR TO BODY TEMPERATURE

Heat the mass over low heat while stirring, and occasionally test the mixture with the side of your index finger until the sugar mass feels just as warm as your body temperature.

MASKING/COATING

Coating the top and sides of a cake evenly with cream.

HEATING YOUR PALETTE KNIFE

Bring water to a boil. Immerse the palette knife in the boiling water, and rub it dry with a towel before use.

PEARL SUGAR

Pearl sugar is a Belgian speciality. The pure white granules are very hard. They come in different sizes and are marked with the letter P. P4 is used for a sugar loaf, for example. You can find this sugar at speciality shops that sell baking ingredients.

PICCOLO

A typical Belgian bread roll.

PISTOLET

A typical Belgian round bread bun.

PRICKING/ DOCKING PASTRY

Pricking or docking pastry dough before baking allows the steam to escape.
If you don't prick the dough, the pastry will puff up.

SEMOLINA

This is the Italian name for coarsely milled durum wheat. The term is also used for semolina from other cereals, such as maize.

STAND MIXER

Invest in a good stand mixer that will last for at least 10 years.

TEMPERING

During tempering, the cocoa butter in the chocolate takes on a stable crystalline form. This guarantees a finished product with a hard snap, good shrinkability and a smooth, glossy sheen. Method: take some chocolate that has been melted to 50°C (100°F) and let it cool to 18°C (35°F). How? Pour some of the chocolate onto a cold, clean work surface. Keep the mass in motion by constantly stirring it with a palette knife and a scraper until the chocolate has cooled down to 18°C (35°F). Add this chocolate to the warmer chocolate, which will cool it to 30°C (60°F). The chocolate mass will have a solid, homogeneous texture with good melting properties and a nice sheen. Ideally, chocolate should feel slightly cooler than your body temperature. One way to test if the chocolate has been correctly tempered is to spread a thin layer of chocolate on a sheet of baking paper. If it sets and is shiny, hard and smooth within a couple of minutes, it has been properly tempered.

WHIPPING CAKE BATTER

When beating cake batter, place a moist towel under the mixing bowl. This prevents the bowl from slipping as you stir or whisk.

WHIPPING CREAM

If you use an electric mixer, whip the cream until it is no longer liquid. Continue beating the cream by hand. That way, you have more control and can avoid overwhipping it (into butter).

LIST OF BRITISH AND AMERICAN TERMS

British	American
all-purpose flour or plain flour	all-purpose flour
aubergine	eggplant
baking paper	baking paper, parchment paper
baking sheet or tray	cookie sheet
baking tin	baking pan
biscuit	cookie
bread tin	bread pan
cake tin	cake pan
caster sugar	superfine sugar
cling film	plastic food wrap, Saran wrap
cooking apples	tart, green apples
cornflour	cornstarch
courgette	zucchini
custard	(similar to) pudding
grated	shredded
kitchen paper	paper towel
maize	corn
sliced/flaked almonds	sliced/slivered almonds
tart	open pie
tart tray	tart sheet
wholemeal	wholewheat

KITCHEN ESSENTIALS

OVEN

All types of ovens, both gas or electric (convection, combination ovens), can be used. The oven must be heated properly to ensure your food is baked evenly. To avoid burning, the food should not touch the bottom of the oven. You can prevent this by adding one or two baking trays which are kept separate from each other by a layer of air. The correct oven temperature is just as important as following the recipes to a tee. Buy an oven thermometer so you can see precisely when your oven has reached the right temperature. You should write down the true temperature for each of your oven settings.

Convection oven

A convection or hot-air oven distributes heat evenly throughout the entire oven cavity, making it ideal for baking. The air is heated in a heat exchanger and circulates around the food thanks to a fan. The temperature can be set a little lower in most cases.

Conventional oven

A conventional oven has electrical heating elements at the top and/or bottom which deliver static radiant heat inside the oven cavity. As a result, these ovens take longer to preheat. As warm air rises away from the heat source, you get spontaneous air circulation or natural convection. As a result, the heat is unevenly distributed: the bottom of the oven cavity is not as hot as the top. It is, therefore, vital that you put your food at the right level. Most ovens have four possible levels or tiers, which are each suitable for specific preparations. Conventional ovens usually have the following cooking modes: conventional or top and bottom heat, and grill under heat.

Gas oven

Gas ovens usually work on gas settings or gas mark numbers rather than temperatures. In many ovens, the marks correspond to the following temperatures (based on a gas oven with 8 marks):

mark	temperature
1	135°C (275°F)
2	150°C (300°F)
3	165°C (325°F)
4	175°C (350°F)
5	190°C (375°F)
6	205°C (400°F)
7	220°C (425°F)
8	235°C (450°F)
9	245°C (475°F)
10	260°C (500°F)

Multifunction ovens

Besides conventional wall heating, multifunction ovens have other cooking modes:
- Hot air, grill: the oven has a grill element for crisping, ideal for au gratin or roasting.
- Steam: steam cooking preserves the colour, flavour and texture of dishes.
- Microwave: ideal for warming up something quickly, such as hot milk for coffee or a bottle for a baby.

The above functions can be combined in various ways. More advanced ovens have automatic cooking programmes, with the oven taking the guesswork out of cooking by using the ideal settings for your dish.

UTENSILS

Must-haves: plastic dough scraper, scissors, paring knife, steel whisk, flexible spatula with a stainless-steel blade, brush, wooden spatula, conical sieve, silicone pan scraper, digital scale, ladle, piping bag, piping nozzles, wooden rolling pin, flour sifter, a set of serrated and non-serrated biscuit cutters, measuring cup, fine-mesh sieve, cake rack, pancake pan and saucepan.

The right **baking tin** is obviously of paramount importance. The material from which baking tins or moulds are made is also a factor in even baking. When buying baking tins or moulds, you should also consider the oven in which you will be baking.

Tinned bakeware is well suited for direct-heat convection ovens. There are better alternatives for electric ovens, however.

Aluminium moulds are good heat conductors, making them suitable for all types of ovens.

Dark, black-coated moulds absorb a lot of heat, distributing it directly to the batter, making them ideally suited for electric and convection ovens. When you use them in a gas oven at lowertemperatures, it is better to place them on a higher level in the oven.

Nowadays, moulds with a non-stick coating are increasingly common. Tefal's are considered the best. The thicker sides trap heat better, speeding up the cooking process and reducing energy consumption. You can also remove cakes more easily from these moulds.

The first time you use tinned bakeware, the recommendation is to heat it to baking temperature for about 30 minutes while empty. That way, you'll find it easier to remove your cake from the mould after baking. Remember to slide the tinned moulds onto a rack at the bottom of the oven so the heat from below reaches the batter first and the pastry bakes evenly.

Your basic equipment should consist of five items: baking trays, bread baking tins, cake moulds and rings, baking dishes, and moulds for small pastries such as tartlets. Other items include classic cake tins such as the bundt tin, cake tins and springforms. If you only have one baking tray available but need several, use baking paper. Baking paper can be easily transferred from your work surface onto a baking sheet.

To clean the moulds, immerse them in cold water immediately after baking and let them soak for a while. To prevent scratching, never try to remove stubborn sticky or burnt baking residue from the mould with a sharp object.

The one thing you really should consider investing in, however, is a **stand mixer**. One of the main benefits is that it allows for hands-free baking and prepping, saving you a lot of time and effort. It is best to use a stand mixer with a bowl cover to avoid spills and splashes. The kneader's essential equipment includes a mixing bowl and various attachments such as a beater, a wire whip and a dough hook.

MORNING ROLLS AND BUNS

Whether crusty or soft, all these rolls and buns make for an irresistibly delicious breakfast. Choose something different every time, or put together a varied breakfast buffet with lots of fun options. *Boerkes*, piccolos, bagels... You name it, there's something for everyone to indulge in. What's more, you can elevate your rolls with all kinds of savoury toppings: a fresh homemade pesto, Caesar mayonnaise and chicken, or harissa and hummus for something completely different. A real treat for yourself, your friends and family! You can also freeze any leftover rolls you didn't eat.

SAVOURY TOPPINGS FOR MORNING OR LUNCHTIME BAGELS

SALMON

FOR 4 ROLLS

- 100 G (½ CUP, 3.5 OZ) CHEESE SPREAD, PLAIN
- 5 G (1 TBSP, 0.18 OZ) FRESH CHOPPED DILL
- 20 G (1 TBSP, 0.71 OZ) HORSERADISH PASTE
- 80 G (½ CUP, 2.8 OZ) SMOKED SALMON STRIPS
- 40 G (¼ CUP, 1.41 OZ) FRESH CUCUMBER, CUT INTO HALF MOONS

1. Mix the cheese spread with the dill and horseradish, and spread it on the sandwiches.
2. Garnish with salmon strips and a few slices of cucumber.

HEALTHY (VEGAN)

FOR 4 ROLLS

- 140 G (⅔ CUP, 4.9 OZ) GUACAMOLE (MASHED AVOCADO SEASONED WITH GARLIC AND HERBS)
- 60 G (4 CUPS, 2.1 OZ) CHERRY TOMATOES
- 10 G (¼ CUP, 0.35 OZ) FRESH ROCKET LEAVES
- 10 G (1 TBSP, 0.35 OZ) TOASTED PINE NUTS

1. Spread the guacamole on the rolls.
2. Garnish with two half cherry tomatoes, some rocket leaves and a few pine nuts.

SPICY

FOR 4 ROLLS

- 40 G (3 TBSP, 1.41 OZ) HARISSA (SPICY PASTE OR SAUCE MADE FROM TOMATO PUREE, CARROT, ONION, ALLSPICE, GINGER, CARAWAY, GARLIC AND SMOKED PAPRIKA)
- 40 G (3 TBSP, 1.41 OZ) HUMMUS (MASHED CHICKPEAS FLAVOURED WITH SESAME PASTE, LEMON AND GARLIC)
- 60 G (⅓ CUP, 2.1 OZ) FETA CHEESE
- 30 G (½ CUP, 1.06 OZ) GRATED CARROT OR 4 SLICED RADISHES

1. Mix the harissa with the hummus.
2. Spread it on the sandwiches and garnish with a piece of feta cheese and carrot or radish.

CAESAR

FOR 4 ROLLS

- 80 G (2.8 OZ) CAESAR MAYONNAISE (65 G (4 TBSP, 2.3 OZ) MAYONNAISE MIXED WITH 10 G (1 TBSP, 0.35 OZ) PARMESAN, 5 G (1 TSP, 0.18 OZ) ANCHOVY PASTE AND SOME LEMON JUICE)
- 80 G (2.8 OZ) COOKED CHICKEN-THIGH MEAT CUT INTO PIECES
- 30 G (¼ HEAD, 1.06 OZ) FRESH LETTUCE LEAVES OF YOUR CHOICE
- 5 G (1 TBSP, 0.18 OZ) MINCED CHIVES

1. Spread the Caesar mayonnaise on the sandwiches.
2. Top with the chicken-thigh pieces, lettuce leaves and chives.

HAM SALAD

FOR 4 ROLLS

- 60 G (4 TBSP, 2.1OZ) MAYONNAISE
- ½ HARD-BOILED EGG, CUT INTO PIECES
- 60 G (¼ CUP, 2.1 OZ) FINELY SLICED HAM
- SALT AND PEPPER
- 5 G (1 TBSP, 0.18 OZ) MINCED CHIVES
- 30 G (¼ CUP, 1.06 OZ) GRATED CELERIAC
- 30 G (¼ CUP, 1.06 OZ) FINELY SLICED GHERKINS
- 10 G (1 TBSP, 0.35 OZ) FINELY CHOPPED FRESH PARSLEY

1. Mix the mayonnaise with the egg and ham, and season with some salt, pepper and chives.
2. Spread it on the rolls and garnish with celeriac, gherkin and parsley.

CHEESE

FOR 4 ROLLS

- 40 G (¼ CUP, 1.41 OZ) CHERRY JAM
- 80 G (4 SLICES, 2.8 OZ) MATURE CHEESE
- 30 G (½ BULB, 1.06 OZ) FENNEL SALAD SLICED THINLY

1. Spread the jam on the rolls, and top with the sliced mature cheese.
2. Garnish with fennel salad.

ITALIAN

FOR 4 ROLLS

- 80 G (⅓ CUP, 2.8 OZ) PESTO (SEE PASTRY BASICS, P. 27)
- 120 G (4 SLICES, 4.2 OZ) DRIED HAM CHIFFONADE
- 50 G (4 SLICES, 1.76 OZ) GRILLED COURGETTE
- 10 G (¼ CUP, 0.35 OZ) PARMESAN FLAKES

1. Spread the pesto on the rolls.
2. Garnish with the ham chiffonade, courgette and parmesan.

TIP

Make the pesto the day before so its flavour can develop.

MAKES 8 BOERKES

- 5 G (0.53 OZ) FRESH YEAST OR 2 ½ TSP (0.09 OZ) INSTANT DRY YEAST
- 240 G (1 CUP, 8.5 OZ) WATER
- 140 G (1 CUP, 4.9 OZ) WHOLEMEAL BREAD FLOUR
- 260 G (2 CUP) BREAD FLOUR
- 10 G (1 TBSP, 3.5 OZ) GOOD-QUALITY MARGARINE
- 6 G SALT (1 TSP, 0.21 OZ)
- FLOUR FOR DUSTING THE *BOERKES*

BOERKES PLAIN, WITH NUTS, SULTANAS, OR CURRANTS (VEGAN)

These soft bread buns with bran always taste great with a delicious topping, whether for breakfast or lunch, or even during a picnic.

1. Line a baking tray with baking paper. Preheat the oven to 220°C (425°F).
2. Put the yeast in a large bowl (if fresh yeast, crumble it), add the water, and stir until completely dissolved. Add the rest of the ingredients, and mix everything into a homogeneous mass.
3. Pour out the dough on the work surface, and knead for 8 to 10 minutes until elastic. Let rest for 30 minutes.
4. Weigh out 8 portions of 80 g (2.8 oz). Shape them into round balls, and arrange them on the baking tray. Make sure the dough balls are spaced sufficiently apart. Let rest for 60 to 70 minutes.
5. Dust the *boerkes* with flour, and bake at 220°C (425°F) for 10 to 12 minutes.

TIP

For boerkes *with nuts, sultanas or currants, after kneading add 75 g chopped walnuts with 20 g (2 tbsp, 0.71 oz) of water, or 75 g (½ cup, 2.5 oz) of raisins/currants with 10 g (1 tbsp, 0.35 oz) of water to the dough, and mix. The dough will feel sticky, but the fruit will soak up the water during the first rise. Other than that, the method is the same, except that you need to weigh out portions of 90 g (3.2 oz).*

I often serve these rolls with cheese platters, in which case I halve the weight and bake them for less long.

CRISPY SEEDED OVEN BAGELS (VEGAN)

MAKES 12 BAGELS

- 30 G (1.06 OZ) FRESH YEAST OR 1 TBSP (0.35 OZ) INSTANT DRY YEAST
- 300 G (1 ¼ CUP, 10.6 OZ) COLD WATER 500 G (17.6 OZ) BREAD FLOUR (4 CUPS)
- 10 G (2 TSP) SALT
- 10 G (1 TBSP, 0.35 OZ) GOOD-QUALITY MARGARINE
- 100 G (⅔ CUP, 3.5 OZ) SEEDS OF YOUR CHOICE: SUNFLOWER SEEDS, BLUE POPPY SEEDS, SESAME SEEDS, FLAXSEED, MILLET, OAT FLAKES, PUMPKIN SEEDS

Everyone knows bagels! The delicious bread buns with a hole in the middle that look a bit like a doughnut. While the recipe is very similar to that of Belgian *pistolets*, the dough balls are formed into rings and baked in the oven.

1. Line a baking tray with baking paper, fill a clean spray bottle with water, and preheat the oven to 230°C (450°F).
2. Put the yeast in a large bowl (if fresh yeast, crumble it), add the water, and stir until completely dissolved. Mix in the flour, salt and margarine.
3. Pour out the dough on the work surface, and knead well for 6 to 8 minutes until smooth. Let rest for 20 minutes at room temperature.
4. Divide the dough into 12 portions of 70 g (2.5 oz) each, and shape into balls. Let the dough balls rise for another 15 minutes.
5. Poke a hole in the center of each ball using your thumb. Pick up the bagel, place both thumbs in the hole, and gently stretch the hole to form a ring with a diameter of 10 cm (3.93 in). Spray the top of the bagels with the spray bottle, and press the moist side into the seeds of your choice.
6. Arrange the bagels on the baking tray with some space in between, and let them rise for 60 to 70 minutes.
7. Spray the bagels again with your spray bottle, and bake at 230°C (450°F) for 16 to 18 minutes until crispy.

SOFT ROLLS WITH SUNFLOWER SEEDS AND OMEGA 3 SEED MIX

MAKES 12 ROLLS

- 40 G (1.41 OZ) FRESH YEAST OR 2 ½ TSP (0.53 OZ) INSTANT DRY YEAST
- 160 G (⅔ CUP, 4.9 OZ) WATER
- 525 G (4 ¼ CUPS, 18.5 OZ) BREAD FLOUR
- 20 G (2 TBSP, 0.71 OZ) GOOD-QUALITY MARGARINE
- 10 G (2 TSP, 0.35 OZ) SALT
- 160 G (⅔ CUP, 5.6 OZ) WHOLE MILK
- 10 G (1 TBSP, 0.35 OZ) GRANULATED SUGAR
- 75 G (½ CUP, 2.7 OZ) SUNFLOWER SEEDS

TO GARNISH: SEED MIX:

- 20 G (½ CUP, 0.71 OZ) SESAME SEED
- 20 G (⅛ CUP, 0.71 OZ) FLAXSEED
- 40 G (¼ CUP, 1.41 OZ) SUNFLOWER SEEDS

A soft roll always tastes good. What's more, they are very easy to make. The buns are super soft and fluffy, just the way I like them. Such a tasty treat on Sunday mornings. You can also freeze them.

1. Line a baking tray with baking paper, fill a clean spray bottle with water, and preheat the oven to 230°C (450°F).
2. Put the yeast in a large bowl (if fresh yeast, crumble it), add the milk and water, and stir until dissolved. Add the flour, margarine, sugar and salt, and continue mixing to form a homogeneous mass.
3. Pour out the dough on the work surface and knead well for 6 to 8 minutes until elastic. Transfer the dough back to the bowl.
4. Add 75 g (½ cup, 2.7 oz) of sunflower seeds and mix well. Let rest for 20 minutes at room temperature.
5. Divide the dough into 12 portions of 80 g (2.8 oz) each, and shape into balls. Let the dough balls rest for another 5 minutes, and form into rolls (see The golden rules of baking, p. 21). Spray the rolls with water, and dip them in the seed mixture. Place the rolls close together, and let them rise another 60 minutes.
6. Spray the rolls with water, and bake at 230°C (450°F) for 8 to 9 minutes. Spray again with water immediately after baking.

VEGAN TIP

For a vegan alternative, substitute the milk with almond milk. To add more flavour, lightly toast the 75 g (½ cup, 2.7oz) sunflower seeds in the oven for 5 minutes at 180°C (350°F).

BASIC DOUGH FOR 12 ROLLS

- 30 G (1.06 OZ) FRESH YEAST OR 1 ½ TBSP (0.35 OZ) INSTANT DRY YEAST
- 300 G (1 ¼ CUP, 1.06 OZ) COLD WATER
- 500 G (4 CUPS, 17.6 OZ) BREAD FLOUR
- 10 G (1 TBSP, 0.35 OZ) GOOD-QUALITY MARGARINE
- 10 G (2 TSP, 0.35 OZ) SALT

PICCOLOS AND BARM CAKES (VEGAN)

1. Put the yeast in a large bowl (if fresh yeast, crumble it), add the water, and stir until dissolved. Add the flour, margarine and salt, and continue mixing to form a homogeneous mass.
2. Pour out the dough on the work surface, and knead well for 6 to 8 minutes until elastic.

BARM CAKES

A barm cake is a soft, round, flattish bread from Northwest England. It is similar to the Belgian soft *pistolet*.

1. Line a baking tray with baking paper. Preheat the oven to 230°C (450°F).
2. Shape the dough into a round ball (see The golden rules of baking, p. 21). Let rest for 30 minutes at room temperature.
3. Roll out the dough until 2 cm thick. Cut out squares of about 70 g (2.50 oz). Arrange the square rolls on the baking tray, leaving some space in between them, and let them rise for 70 minutes.
4. Bake the barm cakes for 6 to 8 minutes at 230°C (450°F). The baked barm cakes should still be white after baking.

PICCOLOS

The *piccolo* belongs to the *pistolet* family. Everyone loves this sandwich roll. They taste great with a sweet or savoury topping and can be eaten at any time of day.

1. Line a baking tray with baking paper, fill a clean spray bottle with water, and preheat the oven to 230°C (450 °F).
2. After kneading, let the dough rest at room temperature for 20 minutes.
3. Form the dough into a tight ball (see The golden rules of baking, p. 21), and leave to rise for another 10 minutes.
4. Divide the dough into 12 portions of 70 g (2.50 oz) each, and shape into balls. Let the dough balls rest for another 5 minutes. Form *piccolos* that are about 14 cm long (see The golden rules of baking, p. 21). Arrange the *piccolos* on the baking tray, leaving some space in between them, and let them rise for 70 minutes.
5. Spray the *piccolos* with water, and bake them for about 20 minutes at 230°C (450°F) until crisp. Prop open the oven door with a spatula for the last two minutes, leaving it slightly ajar to let steam escape. The crust will stay crispier as a result.

TIP

If you want to use the piccolos later, briefly pop them into a warm oven (225°C) (435°F) just before serving so the crust is nice and crispy again.

SWEET *KADETJES* (BUNS)

MAKES 18 *KADETJES*

- 70 G (2.5 OZ) FRESH YEAST OR 2 ½ TBSP (0.88 OZ) INSTANT DRY YEAST
- 300 G (1 ¼ CUP, 10.6 OZ) WHOLE MILK
- 1 EGG
- 600 G (4 CUPS, 2.1 OZ) BREAD FLOUR
- 45 G (4 TBSP, 1.59 OZ) GRANULATED SUGAR
- 50 G (4 TBSP, 1.76 OZ) UNSALTED BUTTER, ROOM TEMPERATURE
- 13 G (3 TSP, 0.46 OZ) SALT
- 1 BEATEN EGG

These soft, sweet buns are a riff on Belgian sandwich rolls, but the dough balls are placed close together so they stick.

1. Butter a 20 × 20 cm square baking tin, or line a baking tray with baking paper. Preheat the oven to 225°C (435°F).
2. Put the yeast into a large bowl, and stir in the milk and egg until the yeast has dissolved. Add the flour, sugar, butter and salt, and mix to form a homogeneous mass.
3. Pour out the dough on the work surface, and knead for 6 to 8 minutes until elastic. After kneading, let the dough rest at room temperature for 30 minutes.
4. Divide the dough into 18 portions of 60 g (2.1 oz), shaping them into balls and arranging them snugly in the baking tin in batches of 3. If you don't have a baking tin, place them closer to each other on the baking tray. Let rise for an hour or slightly longer.
5. Brush the *kadetjes* with the egg wash and bake at 225°C (435°F) for 8 to 10 minutes.

SWEET BREAKFAST

All these pastries are simply irresistible and, in my opinion, the staples of any sweet breakfast. Over the years, I have tried all kinds of variations, and I am happy to share them here. Enjoy croissants with an almond frangipane filling, or make them even sweeter with cherries. I've added vegan cruffins, which are tremendously popular and even richer in flavour thanks to delicious nut spreads. Good news also for bakers looking for a quick fix for serving breakfast in bed, for example. The baked pastries can all be frozen, but remember to wrap them carefully in freezer bags to avoid freezer burn. On the day you want to serve the pastries, preheat your oven to 230°C (450°F). Remove the pastries from the freezer and place them on a baking tray. Pop the baking tray with the frozen pastries in the oven for about two minutes. Take them out and let them thaw further at room temperature for about 15 minutes. They will taste like fresh.

MAKES 16 BOULES

- 1 RECIPE RISEN PUFF PASTRY (SEE PASTRY BASICS, P. 24)
- 1 BEATEN EGG
- 400 G (1 ¾ CUP, 14.01 OZ) PASTRY CREAM (SEE PASTRY BASICS, P. 24)
- 250 G (1 ¾ CUP, 8.8 OZ) GRANULATED SUGAR

BOULES *ALSACIENNES*

This addictive pastry, made with viennoise dough, is a variation on the *boule de Berlin* (Berliner or *Krapfen*), which is made with brioche dough.

1. Line a baking tray with baking paper. Preheat the deep fat fryer to 180°C (350 °F).
2. Make the basic dough, and roll it out into a 2.5 mm (1/10 in) thick rectangle measuring 28 × 64 cm (11.02 × 25.2 in). Cut the slice into two strips measuring 14 × 64 cm (5.52 × 25.2 in), and from these strips cut 16 rectangles measuring 14 × 8 cm (5.52 × 3.15 in). Leave these rectangles like this. Brush their edges with the egg wash.
3. Fill a piping bag (with a large non-serrated nozzle) with the pastry cream. Pipe a thick glob of pastry cream at the top into the centre of the rectangles. Make sure to leave 1.5 cm (0.59 in) free on either side. Roll up the rectangles from top to bottom. Press the sides as you roll.
4. Place the dough rectangles with the seam facing down on a floured towel. Press them down firmly, and leave them to rise for an hour.
5. Carefully place the boules in the frying fat, first with the bottom side up, and fry each side for three minutes until golden brown.
6. Take them out of the fat, and dip them in the granulated sugar.

> **TIP**
>
> *When making boules with jam, use a solid-set jam so that it does not leak while baking.*

MAKES 16 *RONDELETTES*

- 250 G (1 CUP, 8.8 OZ) PASTRY CREAM (SEE PASTRY BASICS, P. 24)
- 1 RECIPE RISEN PUFF PASTRY (SEE PASTRY BASICS, P. 26)
- 1 BEATEN EGG
- 100 G (⅔ CUP, 3.5 OZ) CHOCOLATE DROPS FOR BAKING
- 200 G (7.1 OZ) FONDANT SUGAR WITH COCOA (SEE PASTRY BASICS, P. 25)
- 200 G (1 ¼ CUP, 7.1 OZ) MILK-CHOCOLATE CURLS (SEE PASTRY BASICS, P. 25)

CREAM AND CHOCOLATE *RONDELETTE*

This pastry is a riff on the chocolate cookie but filled with pastry cream and chocolate.

1. Make the pastry cream beforehand so it can cool.
2. Line a baking tray with baking paper, and preheat the oven to 220°C (400°F).
3. Make the basic dough, and roll it out into a 3 mm thick rectangle measuring 40 × 48 cm (15.75 × 18.9 in). Cut the dough into two sheets measuring 20 × 48 cm (7.87 × 18.9 in). Spread the cream on each piece, but make sure to leave a 3 cm (1.18 in) bare border at the bottom. Brush this border lightly with the egg wash. Sprinkle the chocolate drops over the pastry cream.
4. Starting from the top, roll up each strip into a 48 cm (18.9 in) roll. Make sure the seam at the bottom is in the middle, and press the dough down well.
5. Divide with a chef's knife each roll into eight strips, each 6 cm (2.36 in) long, and place them on the baking tray with the seam facing down. Press and leave to rise for 60 to 70 minutes.
6. Brush the biscuits with the egg wash, and bake at 220°C (400°F) for 12 minutes. Leave to cool. Brush them with fondant sugar, and decorate them with chocolate curls.

SWEET BREAKFAST

ALMOND CROISSANT

This recipe is for a croissant with an almond frangipane filling. This croissant is folded from a square, not rolled from a triangle. Did you know that croissants taste best when eaten within 4 hours of baking?

MAKES 16 CROISSANTS

- 1 RISEN PUFF PASTRY (SEE PASTRY BASICS, P. 26)
- 500 G (2 CUPS, 17.6 OZ) ALMOND FRANGIPANE (SEE PASTRY BASICS, P. 24)
- 1 BEATEN EGG
- 100 G (⅔ CUP, 3.5 OZ) ROASTED SLICED ALMONDS (SEE PASTRY BASICS, P. 26)
- 200 G (7.1 OZ) FONDANT SUGAR (SEE PASTRY BASICS, P. 25)
- 50 G (⅓ CUP, 1.76 OZ) ICING SUGAR

1. Line a baking tray with baking paper, and preheat the oven to 225°C (435°F).
2. Make the basic dough, and roll it out thinly into a 2.5 mm (1/10 in) thick 48 cm (18.9 in) square. Cut this into sixteen 12 cm (4.72 in) squares with a chef's knife.
3. Fill a piping bag (with a large nozzle) with the frangipane and pipe some filling into the centre of each square (30 g (1.06 oz) per croissant). Fold a corner over the filling, and pinch it closed. Fold over the other corner, and tuck it under the dough. Arrange the pieces of dough on the baking tray, press slightly, and let rise for an hour.
4. Brush the croissants with the egg wash, and bake at 225°C (435°F) for 12 minutes. Leave to cool. Brush them with the fondant sugar, and garnish with roasted almonds and icing sugar.

SWEET BREAKFAST

FOR 10 *GALETTES*

- 500 G (17.6 OZ) BASIC BRIOCHE DOUGH (SEE PASTRY BASICS, P. 24)
- 1 BEATEN EGG
- 100 G (7 TBSP, 3.5 OZ) UNSALTED BUTTER FROM THE FRIDGE
- 100 G (½ CUP, 3.5 OZ) GRANULATED SUGAR

GALETTES

What do many people reach for in times of stress, confusion or when their emotions get the best of them? A sweet treat! Make this rich brioche your go-to snack during turbulent times. A sweet, comforting galette…

1. Line two baking trays with baking paper, and preheat the oven to 225°C (435°F).
2. Knead the brioche dough, and let it rest for 30 minutes.
3. Divide the dough into ten 50 g (1.76 oz) portions and shape into balls. Let rest for another 10 minutes.
4. Using a rolling pin, roll out the balls into discs of 12 cm diameter (4.72 in), arrange them on the baking tray, and let rise for another 60 minutes.
5. Brush the dough with the egg wash. Cut the butter into pieces, and arrange them on the dough. Sprinkle the galettes generously with granulated sugar, and bake at 225°C (435°F) for 7 to 9 minutes.

CHERRY CROISSANT

MAKES 16 CROISSANTS

- 1 RISEN PUFF PASTRY (SEE PASTRY BASICS, P. 26)
- 250 G (1 CUP, 8.8 OZ) ALMOND FRANGIPANE (SEE PASTRY BASICS, P. 24)
- 250 G (2 CUPS, 8.8 OZ) DARK CHERRIES (DRAINED)
- 1 BEATEN EGG
- 125 G (4.4 OZ) APRICOT JAM FOR DECORATING (SEE PASTRY BASICS, P. 24)
- 200 G (7.1 OZ) FONDANT SUGAR (SEE PASTRY BASICS, P. 25)

This croissant has a sweet-and-sour filling of almond frangipane and cherries. It is folded from a square, not rolled from a triangle.

1. Line a baking tray with baking paper, and preheat the oven to 225°C (435°F).
2. Make the basic dough, and roll it out thinly into a 2.5 mm (1/10 in) thick 48 cm (18.9 in) square. Cut sixteen 12 cm (4.72 in) squares with a chef's knife.
3. Mix the frangipane with the well-drained cherries. Fill a piping bag (with a large nozzle) with the filling, and pipe some filling into the centre of each square (30 g (1.06 oz) per croissant). Fold a corner over the filling, and pinch it closed. Fold over the other corner, and tuck it under the dough. Arrange the pieces of dough on the baking tray, press slightly, and let them rise for another 60 minutes.
4. Brush the croissants with the egg wash, and bake for 12 minutes in an oven at 225°C (435°F). Leave to cool. Brush the baked croissants with apricot jam and the fondant sugar.

TIP

Instead of cherries, you can also add pineapple or apricot in syrup to the frangipane.

CHOCOLATE *POCHE*

MAKES 16 *POCHES*

- 400 G (1 ¾ CUP, 14.01 OZ) PASTRY CREAM (SEE PASTRY BASICS, P. 24)
- 1 RISEN PUFF PASTRY (SEE PASTRY BASICS, P. 26)
- 10 G (2 TSP, 0.35 OZ) COCOA POWDER
- BEATEN EGG
- 300 G (10.6 OZ) FONDANT SUGAR WITH COCOA (SEE PASTRY BASICS, P. 25)

Definitely my favourite pastry. In most recipes, pastry cream is added to the pastry after baking, but in this instance, it is baked with the pastry.

1. Make the pastry cream, and let it cool.
2. Line a baking tray with baking paper, and preheat the oven to 225°C (435°F).
3. Make the basic dough, and roll it out into a 3.5 mm (⅛ in) thick rectangle measuring 30 × 40 cm (11.81 × 15.75 in). Cut the dough into two sheets of 15 × 40 cm (5.9 × 15.75 in).
4. Mix the cocoa powder with the cold pastry cream, and fill a piping bag (with a large non-serrated nozzle) with the mixture. Pipe a thick cylinder of the filling into the centre of each sheet along the entire length (200 g (7.1 oz) of pastry cream per sheet).
5. Lightly brush the top and bottom of the dough with the egg wash, and fold the top half onto the bottom half. Press firmly. Divide each into 8 pieces with a chef's knife, each measuring 5 cm (1.97 in) wide, and arrange them on a baking tray. Let rise for an hour.
6. Brush the pastries with the egg wash, and bake for 12 minutes at 225°C (435°F). Let them cool, and spread fondant sugar on the top of each pastry.

TIP

Substitute pastry cream with frangipane or with walnut, hazelnut or pecan paste (see Pastry basics, pp. 27 & 29). You can also omit the cocoa powder.

Always use a chef's knife to cut or divide.

SESAME AND CHOCOLATE *VIENNOISE*

This Jewish delicacy with chocolate and sesame seeds is very popular around the world, which is why there are quite a few variations of it. The twisted cake is related to the Hungarian *kifli*, the Austrian *kipferl* and the Polish *rogaliki* or *rugelach*. You could say it's a forerunner of the ever-popular croissant.

MAKES 16 SESAME AND CHOCOLATE *VIENNOISES*

- 300 G (10.6 OZ) CHOCOLATE PASTE (SEE PASTRY BASICS, P. 25)
- 1 RISEN PUFF PASTRY (SEE PASTRY BASICS, P. 26)
- 1 BEATEN EGG
- 50 G (⅓ CUP, 1.76 OZ) HULLED/PEELED SESAME SEEDS
- 30 G (¼ CUP, 1.06 OZ) ICING SUGAR

1. Make the chocolate paste one hour beforehand so it can set.
2. Line a baking tray with baking paper, and preheat the oven to 220°C (425°F).
3. Make the basic dough, and roll it out into a 3 mm (⅛ in) thick rectangle measuring 40 × 56 cm (15.75 × 22.04 in). Cut the dough into two sheets measuring 20 × 56 cm (7.87 × 2.04 in).
4. Spread chocolate paste on each sheet, making sure to leave a 3 cm (1.18 in) border at the bottom that is not covered with the spread. Brush it lightly with the egg wash.
5. Starting from the top, roll up each sheet into a 56 cm (22.04 in) roll. Make sure the seam at the bottom is in the middle, and press the dough down well.
6. Divide each roll into 8 small rolls with a chef's knife, each measuring 7 cm (2.76 in). Brush the top of each roll with the egg wash, and dip it in the sesame seeds.
7. Place them on the baking tray with the seam facing down. Press and leave to rise for 60 to 70 minutes.
8. Bake the chocolate viennoise at 220°C (425°F) for 12 minutes. Remove from the oven, let cool, and sprinkle with icing sugar.

ROUND *SUISSE* WITH RAISINS

MAKES 16 *SUISSES*

- 250 G (1 CUP, 8.8 OZ) PASTRY CREAM (SEE PASTRY BASICS, P. 24)
- 1 RISEN PUFF PASTRY (SEE PASTRY BASICS, P. 26)
- 125 G (1 CUP, 4.5 OZ) RAISINS
- 1 BEATEN EGG
- 125 G (4.5 OZ) APRICOT JAM FOR DECORATING (SEE PASTRY BASICS, P. 24)
- 200 G (7.1 OZ) FONDANT SUGAR (SEE PASTRY BASICS, P. 25)

These are also sometimes called escargots. Known in some countries as *pain suisse*, they are spiral-shaped, made of puff pastry, and filled with raisins and pastry cream.

1. Make the pastry cream beforehand so it can cool.
2. Line a baking tray with baking paper, and preheat the oven to 225°C (435 °F).
3. Make the basic dough, and roll it out thinly into a 3 mm (⅛ in) thick 40 × 40 cm (15.75 in) square.
4. Spread the pastry cream on top, making sure to keep a 4 cm (1.58 in) border at the bottom. Press it down with your fingers so it sticks to the table. Sprinkle the sultanas on top of the cream.
5. Form a tight roll, rolling the dough from top to bottom until you reach the bare edge. Brush some egg wash on the top of the roll along the entire length, and continue to roll it up.
6. Using a chef's knife, cut 16 pieces, each 2.5 cm (1 in) wide. Place them on their sides on the baking tray, and leave to rise for another hour.
7. Brush the *suisse* with the egg wash, and bake at 225°C (435 °F) for 12 minutes. After cooling, brush with the jam and then with fondant sugar.

TIP

If you don't like sultanas, you can substitute them with chocolate drops for baking.

SWEET BREAKFAST

STREUSEL BRIOCHE

MAKES 10 BRIOCHES

- 500 G (17.6 OZ) BASIC BRIOCHE DOUGH (SEE PASTRY BASICS, P. 24)
- 5 G (1 TSP, 0.18 OZ) CINNAMON
- 100 G (⅔ CUP, 3.5 OZ) PEARL SUGAR (P4)
- 1 BEATEN EGG
- 100 G (3.5 OZ) STREUSEL (SEE PASTRY BASICS, P. 28)

This delicious streusel brioche smells like speculoos. If you want to make some children very happy, then look no further!

1. Line a baking tray with baking paper, and preheat the oven to 225°C (435°F).
2. Knead the basic dough, and add the cinnamon. After kneading, mix in the pearl sugar. Let rest for half an hour.
3. Weigh out portions of 60 g (2.1 oz), and shape into balls. Place them on the baking tray, and let them rise for 60 to 70 minutes.
4. Brush the tops of the dough balls with the egg wash, and decorate liberally with the streusel. Bake the brioches at 225°C (435°F) for 7 to 8 minutes.

BOURBON VANILLA BRIOCHE

MAKES 10 BRIOCHES

- 500 G (17.6 OZ) BASIC BRIOCHE DOUGH (SEE PASTRY BASICS, P. 24)
- 10 G (2 TSP, 0.35 OZ) VANILLA SUGAR
- 100 G (⅔ CUP, 3.5 OZ) PEARL SUGAR (P4)
- 1 BEATEN EGG

This brioche is sometimes also called *brioche belge*, because Belgians love pearl sugar.

1. Line a baking tray with baking paper, and preheat the oven to 225°C (435°F).
2. Knead the basic dough, and add in the vanilla sugar. After kneading, mix in the pearl sugar. Let rest for half an hour.
3. Weigh out portions of 60 g (2.1 oz), and shape into balls. Place them on the baking tray, and let them rise for 60 to 70 minutes.
4. Brush the tops of the balls with the egg wash, and bake the brioches at 225°C (435°C) for 7 to 8 minutes.

MAKES 10 *MARITOZZI*

- 500 G (17.6 OZ) BASIC BRIOCHE DOUGH (SEE PASTRY BASICS, P. 24)
- 1 BEATEN EGG
- 350 G (12.3 OZ) CHANTILLY CREAM (SEE PASTRY BASICS, P. 27)
- 50 G (⅖ CUP, 1.76 OZ) ICING SUGAR

MARITOZZO

Sweet Roman rolls filled with cream and *amore*. These brioches are a variation on Belgian sandwich rolls and are filled with whipped cream.

1. Line a baking tray with baking paper, and preheat the oven to 225°C (435°F).
2. Knead the basic dough, and let it rest for half an hour.
3. Weigh out ten 50 g (1.76 oz) portions, and shape into balls. Place them on the baking tray, and let them rise for 60 to 70 minutes.
4. Brush the brioches with the egg wash, and bake for 7 to 8 minutes.
5. Let the brioches cool completely. Then slice into them diagonally without cutting all the way through. Fill them with Chantilly cream, and then smooth out the cream over the opening of the bun. Dust with icing sugar.

SUGAR KNOT

MAKES 10 SUGAR KNOTS

- 500 G (17.6 OZ) BASIC BRIOCHE DOUGH (SEE PASTRY BASICS, P. 24)
- 30 G (2 TBSP, 1.06 OZ) SOFT BUTTER
- 300 G (1 ½ CUP, 10.6 OZ) SHINY DECORATING SUGAR

A simple and dainty 'braided' treat for a gentle and dreamy awakening during a Sunday brunch.

1. Line a baking tray with baking paper, and preheat the oven to 220°C (425°F).
2. Knead the basic dough, and let it rest for half an hour.
3. Divide into ten 50 g (1.76 oz) portions. Shape into balls, and then roll them out into 9 cm (3.45 in) long strips. Let the strips rest for 2 minutes, then brush them with butter. The dough will absorb more sugar while you roll it up.
4. Place a towel on the work surface, and sprinkle the shiny decorating sugar on it. Slowly roll out the pieces while pressing them into the decorating sugar (you need about 20 g (0.71 oz)), and form a 25 cm (9.84 in) long strip. You will not need all the sugar.
5. Form a braid. Do this as follows: fold one end of the strip over the other (forming the Greek letter alpha). Fold the bottom end to the top, and stick it through the middle of the dough until the dough comes out at the bottom. Fold the top end under the dough, and pinch it so it sticks to the strips of dough that come out at the bottom. Place the braid on the baking tray, and press it down briefly. Let rise for another hour.
6. Bake the brioches at 220°C (425°F) for 7 to 8 minutes.

FILLED *MASTEL*

A soft brioche with the filling of your choice. The combinations are endless, with fruit, nut spreads, chocolate and cream fillings. You can also make a bunch of different ones. Prepare to fight for the last one in that case.

BLUEBERRY *MASTEL*

- 500 G (17.6 OZ) BASIC BRIOCHE DOUGH (SEE PASTRY BASICS, P. 24)
- 175 G (1 ¼ CUP, 0.62 OZ) FROZEN BLUEBERRIES
- 75 G (2.5 OZ) PIE SAUCE (SEE PASTRY BASICS, P. 28)
- 1 BEATEN EGG
- 10 G (0.35 OZ) STREUSEL (SEE PASTRY BASICS, P. 28)

1. Put the frozen blueberries in a colander, thaw them out, and drain them well.
2. Make the pie sauce, and mix in the blueberries. Set aside to cool
3. Line a baking tray with baking paper, and preheat the oven to 225°C (435°F).
4. Prepare the basic dough, and let it rest for 30 minutes. Divide into ten 50 g (1.75 oz) portions, shape into balls, place on the baking tray, and let rest for 30 minutes.
5. After 30 minutes, press a deep dimple into the dough balls. Use a small herb jar for this. Brush them with the egg wash, and sprinkle some streusel around the edge.
6. Fill each dimple with a generous amount of the blueberry filling. Use a piping bag with a large non-serrated nozzle. Let rise for another 40 minutes.
7. Bake the blueberry *mastels* at 225°C (435°F) for 8 minutes until golden brown.

CHERRY *MASTEL*

- 500 G (17.6 OZ) BASIC BRIOCHE DOUGH (SEE PASTRY BASICS, P. 24)
- 175 G (1 ⅓ CUP, 6.2 OZ) DRAINED DARK CHERRIES IN SYRUP
- 75 G (2.5 OZ) PIE SAUCE (SEE PASTRY BASICS, P. 28)
- 1 BEATEN EGG
- 10 G (0.35 OZ) BUTTER CRUMBLE (SEE PASTRY BASICS, P. 25)

1. Put the cherries in a colander, and let them drain.
2. Make the pie sauce, and mix in the cherries. Set aside to cool
3. Line a baking tray with baking paper, and preheat the oven to 225°C (435°F).
4. Prepare the basic dough, and let it rest for 30 minutes. Divide into ten 50 g (1.75 oz) portions, shape into balls, place on the baking tray, and let rest for 30 minutes.
5. After 30 minutes, press a deep dimple into the dough balls. Use a small herb jar for this. Brush them with the egg wash, and sprinkle the crumble around the edge.
6. Fill each dimple with a generous amount of the cherry filling. Use a piping bag with a large non-serrated nozzle. Let rise for another 40 minutes.
7. Bake the cherry *mastels* at 225°C (435°F) for 8 minutes until golden brown.

ALMOND *MASTEL*

- 500 G (17.6 OZ) BASIC BRIOCHE DOUGH (SEE PASTRY BASICS, P. 24)
- 1 BEATEN EGG
- 75 G (⅔ CUP, 2.5 OZ) SLICED ALMONDS
- 250 G (8.8 OZ) ALMOND FRANGIPANE (SEE PASTRY BASICS, P. 24)

1. Line a baking tray with baking paper, and preheat the oven to 225°C (435°F).
2. Prepare the basic dough, and let it rest for 30 minutes. Divide into ten 50 g (1.75 oz) portions, shape into balls, place on the baking tray, and let rest for 30 minutes.
3. After 30 minutes, press a deep dimple into the dough balls. Use a small herb jar for this. Brush them with the egg wash, and sprinkle the sliced almonds around the edge.
4. Fill each dimple with a generous amount of almond frangipane. Use a piping bag with a large non-serrated nozzle. Let rise for another 40 minutes.
5. Bake the almond *mastels* at 225°C (435°F) for 8 minutes until golden brown.

CREAM *MASTEL*

- 500 G (17.6 OZ) BASIC BRIOCHE DOUGH (SEE PASTRY BASICS, P. 24)
- 1 BEATEN EGG
- 100 G (½ CUP, 3.5 OZ) SHINY DECORATING SUGAR
- 250 G (1 CUP, 8.8 OZ) PASTRY CREAM (SEE PASTRY BASICS, P. 24)

1. Line a baking tray with baking paper, and preheat the oven to 225°C (435°F).
2. Prepare the basic dough, and let it rest for 30 minutes. Divide into ten 50 g (1.76 oz) portions, shape into balls, place on the baking tray, and let rest for 30 minutes.
3. After 30 minutes, press a deep dimple into the dough balls. Use a small herb jar for this. Brush them with the egg wash, and sprinkle the shiny decorating sugar around the edge.
4. Fill each dimple with a generous amount of the pastry cream. Use a piping bag with a large non-serrated nozzle. Let rise for another 40 minutes.
5. Bake the cream *mastels* at 225°C (435°F) for 8 minutes until golden brown.

CHOCOLATE *MASTEL*

- 500 G (17.6 OZ) BASIC BRIOCHE DOUGH (SEE PASTRY BASICS, P. 24)
- 1 BEATEN EGG
- 100 G (⅔ CUP, 3.5 OZ) CHOPPED WALNUTS
- 250 G (8.8 OZ) CHOCOLATE PASTE (SEE PASTRY BASICS, P. 25)

1. Line a baking tray with baking paper, and preheat the oven to 225°C (435°F).
2. Prepare the basic dough, and let it rest for 30 minutes. Divide into ten 50 g (1.76 oz) portions, shape into balls, place on the baking tray, and let rest for 30 minutes.
3. After 30 minutes, press a deep dimple into the dough balls. Use a small herb jar for this. Brush them with the egg wash, and sprinkle the chopped walnuts around the edge.
4. Fill each dimple with a generous amount of the chocolate paste. Use a piping bag with a large non-serrated nozzle. Let rise for another 40 minutes.
5. Bake the chocolate *mastels* at 225°C (435°F) for 8 minutes until golden brown.

CREAM BRIOCHE

MAKES 10 CREAM BRIOCHES

- 500 G (17.6 OZ) BASIC BRIOCHE DOUGH (SEE PASTRY BASICS, P. 24)
- 300 G (1 ¼ CUP, 10.6 OZ) PASTRY CREAM (SEE PASTRY BASICS, P. 24) + 100 G (3.5 OZ) FOR FINISHING
- 100 G (7 TBSP, 3.5 OZ) SOFT UNSALTED BUTTER
- 100 G (½ CUP, 3.5 OZ) CASTER SUGAR
- 1 BEATEN EGG

These stuffed brioches are sometimes compared to little bombs. And rightly so. Both because they are so calorific and because of the explosion of flavour in your mouth when you bite into them.

1. Line a baking tray with baking paper, and preheat the oven to 225°C (435°F).
2. Knead the basic dough, and let it rest for half an hour.
3. Weigh out portions of 50 g (1.76 oz) and shape into balls. Place them on the baking tray, and let them rise for 60 minutes.
4. Fill a piping bag with a small non-serrated nozzle with the pastry cream. Using scissors, cut a small hole into the top of the dough ball. Insert the tip 1 cm (0.39 in) vertically into the brioche, and pipe in the cream (30 grams (1.06 oz) per brioche). Brush the balls with the egg wash, and bake the brioches at 225°C (435°F) for 7 to 8 minutes.
5. Immediately after baking, brush the softened butter onto the brioches and dip them into the granulated sugar. As a finishing touch, pipe some more pastry cream into the hole.

CRUFFINS (VEGAN)

The cruffin is a cross between a croissant and a muffin. It can be filled with all kinds of nut spreads.

TIP

For the non-vegan version, use the basic recipe for risen puff pastry, and add pastry cream and sultanas, chocolate paste, or a non-vegan nut paste.

ALMOND CRUFFIN (VEGAN)

MAKES 16 CRUFFINS

- 1 RECIPE VEGAN RISEN PUFF PASTRY (SEE PASTRY BASICS, P. 26)
- 40 G (3 TBSP, 1.41 OZ) GOOD-QUALITY SOFT MARGARINE
- 80 G (⅖ CUP, 2.8 OZ) GRANULATED SUGAR
- 250 G (1 CUP, 8.8 OZ) VEGAN ALMOND PASTE (SEE PASTRY BASICS, P. 28)

1. Grease 16 serrated muffin tins (Ø 8 cm (3.15 in) and 3 cm (1.18 in) high) generously with margarine, and coat with granulated sugar (5 g (0.18) oz per tin). Preheat the oven to 210°C (415°F).
2. Make the dough, and roll it out into a 3 mm (⅛ in) thick rectangle measuring 25 × 56 cm (9.85 × 22.04 in). Lay the dough lengthwise on the work surface, and spread almond paste on top. Make sure you leave a border of about 4 cm uncovered at the bottom. Press it with your fingers so it sticks to the table.
3. Brush some water on top of the roll along its entire length, and continue rolling. Cut off 3.5 cm (1.37 in) wide pieces, and place them on their sides in the muffin tins. Place the moulds on the baking tray, and leave to rise for another 60 to 70 minutes.
4. Bake the cruffins at 210°C (415°F) for 15 to 18 minutes. After baking, remove them from the mould as soon as you can so they do not stick. Flip them upside down to cool further.

WALNUT CRUFFIN (VEGAN)

MAKES 16 CRUFFINS

- 1 RECIPE VEGAN RISEN PUFF PASTRY (SEE PASTRY BASICS, P. 26)
- 40 G (3 TBSP, 1.41 OZ) GOOD-QUALITY SOFT MARGARINE
- 80 G (⅖ CUP, 2.8 OZ) GRANULATED SUGAR
- 250 G (1 CUP, 8.8 OZ) VEGAN WALNUT PASTE (SEE PASTRY BASICS, P. 29)
- 200 G (7.1 OZ) FONDANT SUGAR (SEE PASTRY BASICS, P. 25)
- 150 G (1 CUP, 5.3 OZ) CHOPPED WALNUTS

1. Grease 16 serrated muffin tins (Ø 8 cm (3.15 in) and 3 cm (1.18 in) high) generously with margarine, and coat with granulated sugar (5 g (0.18 oz) per tin). Preheat the oven to 210°C (415°F).
2. Make the dough, and roll it out into a 3 mm (⅛ in) thick rectangle measuring 25 × 6 cm (9.85 × 22.04 in). Lay the dough lengthwise on the work surface, and spread walnut paste on top. Make sure you leave a strip of about 4 cm uncovered at the bottom. Press it with your fingers so it sticks to the table. Brush some water on top of the roll along its entire length, and continue rolling.
3. Cut off 3.5 cm (1.37 in) wide pieces, and place them on their sides in the muffin tins. Place the moulds on the baking tray, and leave to rise for another 60 to 70 minutes.
4. Bake the cruffins at 210°C (415°F) for 15 to 18 minutes. After baking, remove them from the mould as soon as you can so they do not stick. Flip them upside down to cool further. Brush with the fondant sugar, and garnish with chopped walnuts.

DARK BROWN SUGAR AND CINNAMON CRUFFIN (VEGAN)

MAKES 16 CRUFFINS

- 1 RECIPE VEGAN RISEN PUFF PASTRY (SEE PASTRY BASICS, P. 26)
- 40 G (3 TBSP, 1.41 OZ) GOOD-QUALITY SOFT MARGARINE
- A MIXTURE OF 200 G (1 CUP, 7.1 OZ) DARK BROWN SUGAR AND 100 G (½ CUP, 3.5 OZ) GRANULATED SUGAR
- 1 TSP CINNAMON
- ANOTHER 80 G (⅖ CUP, 2.8 OZ) DARK BROWN SUGAR

1. Grease 16 serrated muffin tins (Ø 8 cm (3.15 in) and 3 cm (1.18 in) high) generously with margarine. Preheat the oven to 210°C (415°F).
2. Make the dough, and roll it out into a 3 mm (⅛ in) thick rectangle measuring 25 × 56 cm (9.85 × 22.04 in). Sprinkle the dough with a generous amount of the sugar mixture. Make sure you leave a border of about 4 cm uncovered at the bottom. Dust the sugar with the cinnamon. Press the uncovered bottom with your fingers so it sticks to the table. Roll (starting at the top) the dough firmly up to the uncovered border.
3. Brush some water on top of the roll along its entire length, and continue rolling. Cut off 3.5 cm (1.37 in) wide pieces. Press one side into the dark brown sugar, and place the cruffins in the muffin tins with the dark brown sugar facing down. Place the moulds on the baking tray, and leave to rise for another 60 to 70 minutes.
4. Bake the cruffins at 210°C (415°F) for 15 to 18 minutes. After baking, remove them from the mould as soon as you can so they do not stick. Flip them upside down to cool further.

PECAN CRUFFIN (VEGAN)

MAKES 16 CRUFFINS

- 1 RECIPE VEGAN RISEN PUFF PASTRY (SEE PASTRY BASICS, P. 26)
- 40 G (3 TBSP, 1.41 OZ) GOOD-QUALITY SOFT MARGARINE
- 80 G (⅖ CUP, 2.8 OZ) GRANULATED SUGAR
- 250 G (1 CUP, 8.8 OZ) VEGAN PECAN PASTE (SEE PASTRY BASICS, P. 29)
- 200 G (7.1 OZ) FONDANT SUGAR (SEE PASTRY BASICS, P. 25)
- 150 G (1 ½ CUP, 5.3 OZ) ROASTED SLICED ALMONDS (SEE PASTRY BASICS, P. 26)

1. Grease 16 serrated muffin tins (Ø 8 cm (3.15 in) and 3 cm (1.18 in) high) generously with margarine, and coat with granulated sugar (5 g (0.18 oz) per tin). Preheat the oven to 210°C (415°F).
2. Make the dough and roll it out into a 3 mm (⅛ in) thick rectangle measuring 25 × 56 cm (9.85 × 22.04 in). Lay it lengthwise on the work surface, and spread pecan paste on top. Make sure you leave a strip of about 4 cm uncovered at the bottom. Press it with your fingers so it sticks to the table. Brush some water on top of the roll along its entire length, and continue rolling.
3. Cut off 3.5 cm (1.37 in) wide pieces, and place them on their sides in the muffin tins. Place the moulds on the baking tray, and leave to rise for another 60 to 70 minutes.
4. Bake the cruffins at 210°C (415°F) for 15 to 18 minutes. After baking, remove them from the mould as soon as you can so they do not stick. Flip them upside down to cool further. Brush them with the fondant sugar, and garnish with the almonds.

NOISETTE

MAKES 16 *NOISETTES*

- 1 RISEN PUFF PASTRY (SEE PASTRY BASICS, P. 26)
- 250 G (1 CUP, 8.8 OZ) HAZELNUT PASTE (SEE PASTRY BASICS, P. 26)
- 1 BEATEN EGG
- 125 G (¾ CUP, 4.5 OZ) CHOPPED WALNUTS
- 200 G (7.1 OZ) FONDANT SUGAR (SEE PASTRY BASICS, P. 25)
- 150 G (1 CUP, 5.3 OZ) *BRÉSILIENNE* NUTS (SEE PASTRY BASICS, P. 25)

A pastry with lots of nuts, both in the paste and as a garnish on top. The noisette is very rich in flavour, a little luxurious even.

1. Line a baking tray with baking paper, and preheat the oven to 220°C (425°F)
2. Make the basic dough, and roll it out into a 3 mm (⅛ in) thick rectangle measuring 40 × 48 cm (15.75 × 18.9 in). Cut the dough into two sheets measuring 20 × 48 cm (7.87 × 18.9 in).
3. Spread the hazelnut paste out on each sheet, but make sure to leave a 3 cm bare border at the bottom. Brush it lightly with the egg wash. Sprinkle the walnut pieces on top of the paste.
4. Roll up each sheet, starting from the top, to form a 48 cm (18.9 in) long roll. Make sure the seam at the bottom of the roll is in the middle, and press the dough firmly.
5. Using a chef's knife, divide each roll into 8 small rolls 6 cm (2.36 in) long, and arrange them on the baking tray with the seam facing down. Press down a little more, and let them rise for another 60 to 70 minutes.
6. Brush the rolls with the egg wash, and bake at 220°C (425°F) for 12 minutes. Leave to cool. Brush them with the fondant sugar, and decorate with the *brésilienne*.

TIP

You can substitute the hazelnut paste with walnut paste or pecan paste (see Pastry basics, pp. 27 & 29).

SUGAR *BOLUS*

MAKES 10 *BOLUSES*

- 20 G (1 ½ TBSP, 0.71 OZ) UNSALTED BUTTER ROOM TEMPERATURE
- 50 G (¼ CUP, 1.76 OZ) GRANULATED SUGAR
- 500 G (17.6 OZ) BASIC BRIOCHE DOUGH (SEE PASTRY BASICS, P. 24)
- 1 BEATEN EGG

This *bolus* is a classic which you can still buy from local bakeries. The bun is made with plain white brioche dough but gets its colour from the caramelised granulated sugar.

1. Butter 10 brioche moulds (Ø 8 cm (3.15 in)) with soft but not runny butter, and coat completely with the granulated sugar. Preheat the oven to 225°C (435°F).
2. Knead the basic dough, and let it rest for half an hour.
3. Weigh out portions of 50 g (1.76 oz) each, and shape into balls. Place the balls in the moulds, and let them rise for 60 to 70 minutes.
4. Brush the tops of the *boluses* with the egg wash, and bake at 225°C (435°F) for 6 to 7 minutes. Bake them for a further 2 minutes with the oven door ajar.
5. After baking, remove them from the mould as soon as you can so they do not stick. Flip them upside down to cool further.

MAKES 10 BRIOCHES

- 500 G (17.6 OZ) BASIC BRIOCHE DOUGH (SEE PASTRY BASICS, P. 24)
- 40 G (3 TBSP, 1.41 OZ) UNSALTED BUTTER, SOFT BUT NOT RUNNY
- 1 BEATEN EGG

BRIOCHE À TÊTE

The classic brioche. It is baked in serrated brioche moulds rather than on a baking tray and consists of a dough ball that is pressed into the mould, with a smaller one on top as a 'head'. Hence its name: *brioche à tête*.

1. Butter 10 brioche moulds (Ø 8 cm (3.15 in)) and preheat the oven to 220°C (425°F).
2. Knead the brioche dough, and let it rest for 30 minutes.
3. Divide the dough into 10 portions of 35 g (1.23 oz) and 10 portions of 15 g (0.53 oz). Roll the 35 g (1.23 oz) portions into firm balls, and place them in the buttered moulds. Let the 15 g (0.53 oz) portions rest on the work surface for 10 minutes.
4. Shape the 15 g (0.53 oz) portions into firm round balls. Moisten your thumb in a glass of water, and press it deep into the centre of the dough in the mould. Stretch the hole open with your fingers, insert the smaller ball, and press. Let rise for another 60 to 70 minutes.
5. Brush the brioches with the egg wash, and bake at 220°C (425°F) for 8 to 10 minutes. After baking, carefully remove them from the moulds.

BREAD AND BUTTER

Is there anything better than waking up to the smell of fresh, home-baked bread at home? Today's world is all about instant gratification and mass production. But when you make bread yourself, you will be amazed at how delicious it can be, and you will be more inclined to start baking every day. When it comes to bread, I find it difficult to pick a favourite, but if I really have to choose, a freshly baked brioche loaf does it for me every time.

BOULDOUK BRIOCHE

This bread, which is said to have been named after the magical rock formations in Cappadocia (Turkey), is simply stunning. In terms of baking technique, it takes its inspiration from *shorgoghal* bread.

SERVES 6

- 500 G (17.6 OZ) BASIC BRIOCHE DOUGH (SEE PASTRY BASICS, P. 24)
- ALL-PURPOSE FLOUR
- 125 G (8 TBSP, 4.5 OZ) UNSALTED BUTTER, ROOM TEMPERATURE
- 10 G (1 ½ TBSP, 0.35 OZ) ICING SUGAR

1. Grease a round tart tray (Ø 22 cm (8.60 in), 4 cm (1.58 in) high) with butter. Preheat the oven to 210°C (410°F).
2. Knead the dough, shape it into a ball, and let it rest for 30 minutes.
3. Dust your work surface with flour, and roll out the dough into a 30 cm (11.81 in) square.
4. Make the butter spreadable, and spread it over two-thirds of the dough. Fold the part without butter to the centre, and fold the other part on top.
5. Place the dough in the fridge for 15 minutes to stiffen.
6. Using a rolling pin, roll out the dough into a sheet measuring 30 × 35 cm (11.81 × 13.78 in)
7. Slowly roll (starting from the top) the dough into a firm 35 cm (13.78 in) long roll. Make sure the seam is facing down.
8. Cut into 7 portions, each 5 cm (1.97 in) wide, and place them on their sides in the baking tin, forming a circle of 6 portions with 1 in the centre. Let rise for another 70 minutes.
9. Bake the *bouldouk* at 210°C (410°F) for 20 to 25 minutes.
10. After baking, remove from the tins, and dust with icing sugar.

WHOLEMEAL FRUIT AND HAZELNUT LOAF (VEGAN)

FOR TWO 600-G (21 OZ) LOAVES

- 25 G (0.88 OZ) FRESH YEAST OR 1 TBSP (0.32 OZ) INSTANT DRY YEAST
- 320 G (1 ⅓ CUP, 11.3 OZ) WATER
- 500 G (4 CUPS, 17.6 OZ) WHOLEMEAL WHEAT FLOUR
- 10 G (1 TBSP, 0.35 OZ) GOOD-QUALITY MARGARINE
- 10 G (2 TSP, 0.35 OZ) SALT
- 120 G (¾ CUP, 4.2 OZ) DRIED FIGS CHOPPED INTO PIECES
- 120 G (¾ CUP, 4.2 OZ) RAISINS
- 120 G (¾ CUP, 4.2 OZ) ROASTED HAZELNUTS (SEE PASTRY BASICS, P. 26)
- 40 G (4 TBSP, 1.41 OZ) EXTRA WATER
- FLOUR FOR DUSTING

This bread is ideal for a healthy breakfast but is equally delicious when served alongside a cheese platter. The combination of mild cheeses, fruits and nuts is simply divine.

1. Line a baking tray with baking paper. Preheat the oven to 225°C (435°F).
2. Put the yeast in a large bowl (if fresh yeast, crumble it), add the water, and stir until completely dissolved. Add the wholemeal wheat flour, margarine and salt, and mix everything to form a homogenous mass.
3. Pour out the dough on the work surface and knead for 6 to 8 minutes until elastic.
4. Add the fruit, nuts and extra water, and mix well. The dough will stick, but during the first rise, the fruit will absorb the moisture. Let the dough rest at room temperature for 30 minutes.
5. Divide the dough into two 600 g (21 oz) portions, shape into a firm ball, and let rest for another 10 minutes.
6. Shape the balls into 25 cm (9.85 in) long loaves (see The golden rules of baking – (Ob)long loaves, p. 20), and let them rise for another 60 minutes.
7. Dust the loaves with flour, and bake for 30 minutes in a 225°C (435°F) oven, turning down the oven temperature to 200°C (400°F)

> **TIP**
>
> *You can also add other types of fruit, including dates, dried apricots, dried plums, and currants. Make sure to respect the total weight.*

VANILLA *BOULOT PERLÉ*

FOR 3 LOAVES (350 G, 12 OZ EACH)

- 65 G (2.3 OZ) FRESH YEAST OR 2 ½ SPOON (22 OZ) INSTANT DRY YEAST
- 125 G (½ CUP, 4.5 OZ) WHOLE MILK, COLD
- 2 LARGE EGGS
- 450 G (3 ¾ CUP, 15.9 OZ) BREAD FLOUR
- 30 G (3 TBSP, 1.06 OZ) GRANULATED SUGAR
- 10 G (2 TSP, 0.35 OZ) VANILLA SUGAR
- 135 G (9 TBSP, 4.8 OZ) UNSALTED BUTTER AT ROOM TEMPERATURE
- 10 G (2 TSP, 0.35 OZ) SALT
- 150 G (1 CUP, 5.3 OZ) COARSE PEARL SUGAR (P4)
- 1 BEATEN EGG

A typical characteristic of this *boulot* bread is its soft, sweet crumb, the result of the melting of the pearl sugar during baking. This bread is also called *craquelin* (Belgian sugar bread). It is a real treat, and you can eat it at any time of the day. Enjoy it with some homemade hot chocolate milk.

1. Line a baking tray with baking paper and preheat the oven to 190°C (375°F).
2. Put the yeast in a large bowl (if fresh yeast, crumble it), add the milk and egg, and stir until dissolved. Add the flour, sugar, vanilla sugar, butter and salt, and continue mixing to form a homogeneous mass.
3. Pour out the dough on the work surface and knead for 8 to 10 minutes until elastic. Check with the windowpane test. You will notice that the dough becomes quite sticky. Do not add flour, but continue kneading until the dough no longer sticks to the work surface. While kneading, the dough sticking to your hands will also be incorporated. Remember to scrape the dough often with a scraper, and work in a room that is not too hot.
4. After kneading, mix in the pearl sugar. Let rest for 15 minutes. Divide the dough into three portions of 350 g (12 oz) each, and shape into firm balls. Let rest for another 15 minutes.
5. Form 20 cm (7.87 in) long large sandwich rolls (see The golden rules of baking - sandwich rolls, p. 21). Arrange them on the baking tray, and let them rise for another 60 to 70 minutes.
6. Brush them with the egg wash, and bake the *boulots* for 20 to 25 minutes in a 190°C (375°F) oven, turning down the oven temperature to 185°C (370°F).

SESAME SANDWICH LOAF (VEGAN)

FOR 2 LOAVES
- 20 G (0.71 OZ) FRESH YEAST OR 2 TSP (0.25 OZ) INSTANT DRY YEAST
- 325 G (1 ⅓ CUP, 11.2 OZ) WATER
- 550 G (4 ⅓ CUP, 1.9 OZ) BREAD FLOUR
- 10 G (1 TBSP, 0.35 OZ) GOOD-QUALITY MARGARINE
- 10 G SALT (2 TSP, 0.35 OZ)
- 30 G (3 TBSP, 1.06 OZ) SOFT MARGARINE
- 80 G (½ CUP, 2.8 OZ) SESAME SEEDS
- FLOUR FOR DUSTING

People have been using sesame seeds in bread since the dawn of time. The practice is said to have originated in ancient Mesopotamia. This makes sesame bread one of the oldest known forms of seeded bread.

1. Preheat the oven to 225°C (435°F).
2. Put the yeast in a large bowl (if fresh yeast, crumble it), add water, and stir until dissolved. Add the flour, the 10 g (0.35 oz) of margarine and the salt, and mix to form a homogeneous mass.
3. Continue kneading the dough on the work surface for about six minutes until elastic. Let rest for 20 minutes.
4. Divide the dough into two portions of 450 g (15.9 oz) each, and let rest for another 20 minutes.
5. Grease 2 rectangular bread tins (1 l capacity) generously with the soft margarine, and coat them with the sesame seeds.
6. Shape the balls into loaves (see The golden rules of baking - (Ob)long loaves, p. 20), and place them seam down in the baking tin. Let rise for another hour.
7. Brush the dough with water, and dust with flour. Make a deep cut in the middle with a sharp knife. Bake the loaves for 30 to 35 minutes in a 225°C (435°F) oven, turning down the oven temperature to 200°C (400°F).

TEAR (AND SHARE) SANDWICH LOAF

FOR TWO 400-G (14.1 OZ) LOAVES

- 40 G (1.41 OZ) FRESH YEAST OR 1 ½ TBSP (14 OZ) INSTANT DRY YEAST
- 225 G (4/5 CUP, 8 OZ) WHOLE MILK
- 1 LARGE EGG
- 425 G (3 CUPS, 14.9 OZ) BREAD FLOUR
- 10 G (2 TSP, 0.35 OZ) SALT
- 65 G (4 TBSP, 2.3 OZ) UNSALTED BUTTER
- 1 BEATEN EGG FOR THE EGG WASH

This is my favourite recipe for bread for toasting. You can easily tear slices off the bread, hence its name.

1. Grease 2 rectangular bread tins (12 × 20 cm (4.72 × 7.87 in) and 1 l capacity) with butter. Preheat the oven to 190°C (375°F).
2. Put the yeast in a large bowl (if fresh yeast, crumble it), add the milk and egg, and stir until dissolved. Mix in the flour, salt and softened butter.
3. Continue kneading the dough on the work surface for 6-8 minutes until elastic. Let rest for 20 minutes.
4. Weigh out 20 portions of 40 g (1.41 oz). Shape them into nice round balls, let them rest for 2 minutes, and then form narrow sandwiches (12 cm (4.72 in) long) (see The golden rules of baking – sandwich rolls, p. 21). Place 10 sandwiches side by side in a row in a baking tin, and repeat for the second loaf. Let them rise for another hour.
5. Brush them with the egg wash, bake at 190°C (375°F) for 25 minutes, and leave to cool.

TIP

The slices are delicious when toasted.

BRIOCHE LOAF WITH CHOCOLATE

MAKES THREE LOAVES, 350 G (12.3 OZ) EACH

- 60 G (2.1 OZ) FRESH YEAST OR 2 ½ TBSP (0.81 OZ) INSTANT DRY YEAST
- 110 G (½ CUP, 3.9 OZ) WHOLE MILK
- 1 ½ LARGE EGG
- 410 G (3 CUPS, 14.5 OZ) BREAD FLOUR
- 30 G (3 TBSP, 1.06 OZ) GRANULATED SUGAR
- 115 G (8 TBSP, 3.41 OZ) SOFT UNSALTED BUTTER
- 8 G (2 TSP, 0.28 OZ) SALT
- 250 G (1 ½ CUP, 8.8 OZ) CHOCOLATE DROPS FOR BAKING
- 1 BEATEN EGG FOR THE EGG WASH
- 50 G (1.76 OZ) FONDANT SUGAR WITH COCOA (SEE PASTRY BASICS, P. 25)
- 50 G (1.76 OZ) CHOCOLATE CURLS (SEE PASTRY BASICS, P. 25)

This classic definitely has to feature on our list of sweet bread. Its intense chocolate flavour makes for an insanely tasty breakfast. The basic dough originally comes from the border region between Belgium, France and Luxembourg, where people have been making it for centuries.

1. Line a baking tray with baking paper. Preheat the oven to 185°C (370°F).
2. Put the yeast in a large bowl (if fresh yeast, crumble it). Add the milk and egg, and stir until dissolved.
3. Mix in the flour, sugar, butter and salt, and continue mixing to form a homogeneous mass.
4. Pour out the dough on the work surface and knead well for 8 to 10 minutes until elastic. Mix in the chocolate drops. At first, the dough will feel sticky. This is because the butter needs more time to be absorbed by the flour. Let rest for 30 minutes at room temperature.
5. Weigh three portions of 350 g (12.3 oz) each, and let them proof for 30 minutes.
6. Knock all the air out of the dough, and shape into balls again. Place them on the baking tray, and let them rise for 60 minutes.
7. Brush the loaves with the egg wash, and bake at 185°C (370°F) for about 20 to 25 minutes. Leave to cool.
8. Brush them with the fondant sugar, and decorate them with the chocolate curls.

RUSTIC *PAIN DE CAMPAGNE*/ COUNTRY LOAF (VEGAN)

FOR TWO LOAVES, 600 G (21 OZ) EACH

- 25 G (0.88 OZ) FRESH YEAST OR 1 TBSP (0.32 OZ) INSTANT DRY YEAST
- 420 G (1 ¾ CUP) WATER
- 275 G (2 CUPS, 9.5 OZ) WHOLEMEAL WHEAT FLOUR
- 445 G (3 ½ CUP) BREAD FLOUR
- 25 G (2 TBSP, 0.88 OZ) GOOD-QUALITY MARGARINE
- 15 G (3 TSP, 0.53 OZ) SALT
- FLOUR FOR DUSTING

This French country bread from the Auvergne region is a classic. Known for its distinctive creative scoring, it has a thicker crust, which helps it stay fresh longer. Pain de campagne can be eaten for breakfast but is also ideal for making toasted sandwiches.

1. Line a baking tray with baking paper. Preheat the oven to 225°C (435°F).
2. Put the yeast in a large bowl (if fresh yeast, crumble it), add the water, and stir until completely dissolved. Add the rest of the ingredients, and mix everything into a homogeneous mass.
3. Pour out the dough on the work surface and knead for 6-8 minutes until smooth. Let rest for 20 minutes at room temperature.
4. Divide the dough into two portions of 600 g (21 oz) each, shape into firm balls, and leave them to rest for another 20 minutes.
5. Using a rolling pin, roll out the dough into round discs (Ø 18 cm), and place them on the baking tray. Allow the loaves to rise for 60 to 70 minutes.
6. Dust the loaves with flour, and score them a few times in two directions with a sharp knife. Bake them for 30 minutes in a 225°C (435°F) oven, turning down the temperature to 200°C (425°F).

> **TIP**
>
> *For a white* pain de campagne, *use the recipe for white bread.*

BRIOCHE DE NANTERRE WITH RAISINS

FOR TWO LOAVES, 500 G (17.6 OZ) EACH
- 60 G (2.1 OZ) FRESH YEAST OR 2 ½ TBSP (0.81 OZ) INSTANT DRY YEAST
- 110 G (½ CUP, 3.9 OZ) WHOLE MILK
- 1 ½ LARGE EGG
- 410 G (3 CUPS, 14.5 OZ) BREAD FLOUR
- 30 G (3 TBSP, 1.06 OZ) GRANULATED SUGAR
- 115 G (8 TBSP, 3.41 OZ) SOFT UNSALTED BUTTER
- 8 G (2 TSP, 0.28 OZ) SALT
- 225 G (1 ½ CUP, 8 OZ) RAISINS
- 1 BEATEN EGG FOR THE EGG WASH

They say this brioche is centuries old. In the fifth century, the archdeacon of Auxerre brought blessed rolls to Saint Geneviève in Nanterre, France. In subsequent centuries, people continued to bring sandwiches to the canons of St Geneviève's abbey. In those days, the saint's effigy would have been pressed into the buns. The top is divided into six to eight equal parts. This delicacy has lost none of its popularity over time.

1. Grease 2 rectangular bread tins (12 × 20 cm (4.72 × 7.87 in) and 1 l capacity) with butter. Preheat the oven to 190°C (375°F).
2. Put the yeast in a large bowl (if fresh yeast, crumble it). Add the milk and egg, and stir until dissolved.
3. Mix in the flour, sugar, butter and salt, and continue mixing to form a homogeneous mass.
4. Pour out the dough on the work surface, and knead well for 8 to 10 minutes until elastic. Mix in the sultanas. At first, the dough will feel sticky. This is because the butter needs more time to be absorbed by the flour. Let rest for 30 minutes at room temperature.
5. Divide the dough into 12 portions of 85 g (3 oz) each. Shape into firm balls, and place 6 of them close together in the baking tin. Let rise for another hour.
6. Brush the brioche with the egg wash, and bake at 190°C (375°F) for about 25 to 30 minutes.
7. After baking, remove the brioche from the mould, and leave to cool on a wire rack.

GALETTE BRIOCHÉE

FOR A 550 G (20 OZ) GALETTE
- SOFT BUTTER FOR SPREADING
- 35 G (1.23 OZ) FRESH YEAST OR 1½ TBSP (0.42 OZ) INSTANT DRY YEAST
- 60 G (¼ CUP, 2.1 OZ) WHOLE MILK
- 1 LARGE EGG
- 230 G (1 ¾ CUP, 8.1 OZ) BREAD FLOUR
- 20 G (2 TBSP, 0.71 OZ) GRANULATED SUGAR
- 70 G (5 TBSP, 2.5 OZ) SOFT UNSALTED BUTTER, ROOM TEMPERATURE
- 4 G (1 TSP, 0.14 OZ) SALT
- 80 G (½ CUP, 2.8 OZ) COARSE PEARL SUGAR (P4)

TO FINISH BEFORE BAKING:
- 1 BEATEN EGG FOR THE EGG WASH
- 30 G (1.06 OZ) UNSALTED BUTTER FROM THE REFRIGERATOR
- 50 G (¼ CUP, 1.76 OZ) GRANULATED SUGAR

'Galette' is French for a round flat pancake or waffle. The base is often a brioche dough, which provides a sweet crust. This galette is popular because it stays fresh for a long time and is quite the energy booster.

1. Generously grease a round tart tray (Ø 20 cm (7.87 in), 4 cm (1.58 in) high) with softened butter. Preheat the oven to 190°C (375°F).
2. Put the yeast in a large bowl (if fresh yeast, crumble it). Add the milk and egg, and stir until dissolved. Mix in the flour, sugar, 70 g (5 tbsp, 2.5 oz) of butter, and salt, and continue mixing to form a homogeneous mass.
3. Pour out the dough on the work surface and knead well for 8 to 10 minutes until elastic. At first, it will feel sticky. This is because the butter needs more time to be absorbed by the flour.
4. Lastly, mix in the pearl sugar. Shape into a ball, and let rest at room temperature for 30 minutes.
5. Using a rolling pin, roll out the dough into a 20 cm (7.87 in) disc, and place it in the cake mould. Let rise for an hour.
6. Brush the dough with the egg wash. Cut the 30 g (1.06 oz) of butter into cubes, and spread them over the dough. Sprinkle generously with the granulated sugar.
7. Bake the galette for 25 to 30 minutes in a 190°C (375°F) oven, turning down the oven temperature to 180°C (350°F).

BREAD AND BUTTER

SOFT NUT *BRETZEL* (VEGAN)

FOR 2 NUT *BRETZELS*, 400 G (14.1 OZ) EACH
- 15 G (0.53 OZ) FRESH YEAST OR 2 TSP (0.20 OZ) INSTANT DRY YEAST
- 215 G (1 CUP, 7.6 OZ) WATER
- 375 G (3 CUP, 13.3 OZ) BREAD FLOUR
- 20 G (2 TBSP, 0.71 OZ) GOOD-QUALITY MARGARINE
- 8 G (2 TSP, 0.28 OZ) SALT
- 170 G (1 ¼ CUP, 6 OZ) CHOPPED WALNUTS
- 15 G (1 ½ TBSP, 0.53 OZ) WATER

When I say *'pretzel'*, most people think of the savoury and amazingly addictive crunchy snack you can buy in supermarkets. But if you've already crossed the German border, you have already tasted its big brother, the *Bretzel*. My version of this bread is a white bread dough filled with nuts. Delicious and healthy!

1. Preheat the oven to 225°C (435°F).
2. Put the yeast in a large bowl (if fresh yeast, crumble it). Add water and stir until dissolved. Add the flour, margarine and salt, and mix to form a homogeneous mass.
3. Pour out the dough on the work surface and knead for 6 minutes until elastic. Mix in the nuts along with 15 g (1 ½ tbsp, 0.53 oz) of water. The dough will feel sticky to the touch, but the nuts will absorb the moisture while resting. Let rest for 20 minutes at room temperature.
4. Divide the dough into two portions of 400 g (14.1 oz) each, and shape into 25 cm (9.85 in) long portions (see The golden rules of baking - (Ob)long loaves, p. 20). Let the dough rest for another 10 minutes.
5. Roll the portions into 90 cm (35.4 in) long strips, and make a mark in the dough 40 cm (15.75 in) starting from the right and 40 cm (15.75 in) starting from the left. Now turn the right section towards the left mark, and press it firmly into the dough. Turn the left section onto the right mark, and press it down too. Flip the *Bretzel* over, and place it on the baking tray. Let it rise for another hour.
6. Bake the *Bretzel* at 225°C (435°F) for about 10 minutes.

COUQUE CHIFFON

FOR 1 *CHIFFON* LOAF

- 25 G (0.88 OZ) FRESH YEAST OR 1 TBSP (0.32 OZ) INSTANT DRY YEAST
- 80 G (¼ CUP, 2.8 OZ) WHOLE MILK
- ½ LARGE EGG
- 185 G (1 ½ CUP, 6.5 OZ) BREAD FLOUR
- 15 G (1 TBSP, 0.53 OZ) UNSALTED BUTTER, ROOM TEMPERATURE
- 15 G (3 TSP, 0.53 OZ) GRANULATED SUGAR
- 4 G (1 TSP, 0.14 OZ) SALT
- 35 G (¼ CUP, 1.23 OZ) COARSE PEARL SUGAR (P4)
- 75 G (½ CUP, 2.7 OZ) CHOCOLATE (CHOPPED) FOR BAKING
- SOFT BUTTER FOR THE BAKING TIN
- 40 G (⅓ CUP, 1.41 OZ) SLICED ALMONDS
- 10 G (1 ½ TBSP, 0.35 OZ) ICING SUGAR

I made this delicious bundt once for Christmas and it was an instant hit. This sweet bread has become a tradition in my family, and we also often make it for breakfast during the year.

1. Preheat the oven to 190°C (375°F)
2. Put the yeast in a large bowl (if fresh yeast, crumble it), add the milk and egg, and stir until dissolved. Mix in the flour, butter, sugar and salt.
3. Pour out the dough on the work surface, and knead for 6 to 8 minutes until elastic. Check with the windowpane test. You will notice that the dough becomes quite sticky. Do not add flour, but continue kneading until the dough no longer sticks to the work surface. While kneading, the dough sticking to your hands will also be incorporated. Remember to scrape the dough often with a scraper, and work in a room that is not too hot.
4. Mix the pearl sugar and chocolate (chopped) into the dough, and leave to rest for 30 minutes.
5. Grease a bundt tin (Ø 22 cm (8.60 in), 6 cm (2.36 in) high) with softened butter, and coat it with the almonds.
6. Make the dough 40 cm (15.75 in) long (see The golden rules of baking - (Ob) long sandwiches, p. 20), and place it in the bundt with the ends of the long sandwich roll pressed together. Press down lightly.
7. Let rise for an hour, and bake the *chiffon* loaf for 25 to 30 minutes in a 190°C (375°F) oven, turning down the oven temperature to 185°C (370°F).
8. After baking, turn the *chiffon* loaf out onto a wire rack and leave to cool. Dust with icing sugar.

SEMOLINA *FALUCHE* (VEGAN)

MAKES 6 *FALUCHES*

- 25 G (0.88 OZ) FRESH YEAST OR 1 TBSP (0.32 OZ) INSTANT DRY YEAST
- 330 G (1 ⅓ CUP, 11.6 OZ) WATER
- 540 G (4 CUPS, 19 OZ) SEMOLINA (DURUM WHEAT SEMOLINA)
- 10 G (1 TBSP, 0.35 OZ) SUGAR
- 10 G (2 TSP, 0.5 OZ) SALT
- 100 G (⅔ CUP, 3.5 OZ) SEMOLINA FOR FINISHING THE *FALUCHE*
- FLOUR FOR DUSTING

A *faluche* is a traditional bread from northern France. I made my own version with semolina. When I go surfing in Dakhla in Morocco, the *smida,* made with semolina, is my favourite breakfast staple. I learned how to make it from my hostess.

1. Line a baking tray with baking paper. Preheat the oven to 230°C (440°F).
2. Put the yeast in a large bowl (if fresh yeast, crumble it). Add water and stir until dissolved. Add the semolina, sugar and salt, and mix to form a homogeneous mass.
3. Pour out the dough on the work surface, and knead well for 6 to 8 minutes until elastic. Kneading will feel different because you are using semolina, not wheat flour.
4. Divide into 6 portions of 150 g (5.3 oz) each, and shape into 15 cm (5.90 in) long rolls. Let rest for another 30 minutes.
5. Spread 100 g (⅔ cup, 3.5 oz) of semolina on a clean towel. Use your hands to flatten the *faluches* in the semolina (8 × 20 cm (3.15 × 7.87 in)). Place them on the baking tray, and let them rise for another 70 minutes.
6. Press 10 dimples into the dough with two fingers, and bake at 230°C (440°F) for 8 to 10 minutes.

BREAD AND BUTTER

BABKALLAH

MAKES 2 LOAVES

- 60 G (2.1 OZ) FRESH YEAST OR 2 ½ TBSP (0.81 OZ) INSTANT DRY YEAST
- 100 G (⅖ CUP, 3.5 OZ) WHOLE MILK
- 1 ½ LARGE EGG
- 410 G (3 CUPS, 14.5 OZ) BREAD FLOUR
- 30 G (3 TBSP, 1.06 OZ) GRANULATED SUGAR
- 115 G (8 TBSP, 3.41 OZ) SOFT UNSALTED BUTTER
- 8 G (2 TSP, 0.28 OZ) SALT
- 250 G (8.8 OZ) CHOCOLATE PASTE (SEE PASTRY BASICS, P. 25)
- ½ TEASPOON CINNAMON
- 1 BEATEN EGG
- 40 G (1.41 OZ) SUGAR SYRUP (SEE PASTRY BASICS, P. 27)

Babkallah is a delicious chocolate and cinnamon plaited brioche loaf. This trendy bread is quite easy to make. Don't be afraid of getting creative for some surprising results!

BREAD AND BUTTER

1. Grease two loaf moulds (12 × 20 cm (4.72 × 7.87 in) and 1 l capacity) with butter, and line them with baking paper. Preheat the oven to 190°C (375°F).
2. Put the yeast in a large bowl (if fresh yeast, crumble it). Add the milk and egg, and stir until dissolved. Add the flour, butter, sugar and salt, and continue mixing to form a homogeneous mass.
3. Pour out the dough on the work surface, and knead well for 6 to 8 minutes until elastic. Let rest for half an hour.
4. On a lightly floured work surface, roll out the dough into a 3 mm thick (⅛ in) square (40 cm (15.72 in)).
5. Spread with a generous amount of the chocolate paste, and sprinkle with some cinnamon.
6. Carefully roll the dough into a 40 cm (15.72 in) long roll, and refrigerate for 15 minutes to stiffen.
7. Cut the roll lengthwise into two halves. Place one half over the other half to form a braid until you reach the end. Pinch the top and bottom well. Cut the braid in half, and place the two halves in the baking moulds. Let rise for another hour.
8. Brush the *babkallah* with the egg wash, and bake at 190°C (375°F) for 25 to 30 minutes.
9. Brush with syrup immediately after baking.

TIP

You can sprinkle some chopped walnuts on top of the chocolate paste for a fun twist or replace the chocolate paste with walnut, pecan, or hazelnut paste (see pastry basics, pp. 27–29).

PAGNON AMANDE

FOR A 750 G (27 OZ) BRIOCHE

- 35 G (1.23 OZ) FRESH YEAST OR 1 ½ TBSP (0.42 OZ) INSTANT DRY YEAST
- 100 G (⅖ CUP, 3.5 OZ) WHOLE MILK
- 1 ½ LARGE EGG
- 210 G (1 ½ CUP, 7.4 OZ) BREAD FLOUR
- 15 G (1 ½ TBSP, 5.3 OZ) GRANULATED SUGAR
- 5 G (1 TBS, 0.18 OZ) SALT
- 20 G (1 TBSP, 0.71 OZ) UNSALTED BUTTER, ROOM TEMPERATURE
- 250 G (1 CUP, 8.8 OZ) ALMOND FRANGIPANE (SEE PASTRY BASICS, P. 24)
- 125 G (⅘ CUP, 4.5 OZ) CHOPPED WALNUTS
- 1 BEATEN EGG FOR THE EGG WASH
- 40 G (⅙ CUP, 1.41 OZ) FRESH CREAM CHEESE
- 100 G (1 ¼, 3.5 OZ) ICING SUGAR

I went all out for this bread! The almond frangipane and nut filling adds an irresistible twist to this soft brioche bread. Time to get creative yourself with this *swirl* bread!

1. Grease a springform (Ø 18 cm (7.08 in) and 6 to 7 cm (2.36 to 2.76 in) high) with butter. Preheat the oven to 185°C (370°F).
2. Put the yeast in a large bowl (if fresh yeast, crumble it), add the milk and egg, and stir until dissolved. Add the flour with the sugar, salt and butter.
3. Pour out the dough on the work surface, and knead for 6 to 8 minutes until elastic. Check with the windowpane test. You will notice that the dough becomes quite sticky. Do not add flour, but continue kneading until the dough no longer sticks to the work surface. Remember to scrape the dough often with a scraper, and work in a room that is not too hot.
4. Let the kneaded dough rest for half an hour.
5. Using a rolling pin, roll out the dough into a 20 × 45 cm (7.87 × 17.72 in) rectangle, and cut this into four 5 × 45 cm (1.97 × 17.72 in) strips.
6. Spread ¼ of the frangipane on a strip, and sprinkle nuts on top. Place a second strip on top of the first one, and spread frangipane on it too, topping it with nuts. Do the same with strip 3 and strip 4.
7. Roll the thick strip into a large round galette, and place it in the springform. Press the dough firmly, and leave to rise for 60 to 70 minutes.
8. Brush with the egg wash, and bake for 35 to 40 minutes.
9. Open the springform, remove the pagnon, and leave to cool.
10. While stirring, melt the soft cream cheese in a pan over low heat. Add the icing sugar, and continue to stir until a liquid glaze forms. This takes very little time. Make sure the mixture is never hotter than your body temperature. Check the temperature regularly with your finger. Brush the cake with the mixture, and leave to set.

ON THE CAKE STAND

All the cakes and tarts in this chapter have one thing in common: they are all equally delicious. Take a bite, and you won't be able to stop! You will find many of my classic recipes here, as well as some cakes that are inspired by international recipes, such as the blueberry cheesecake. Some recipes take a bit more time and require patience as they need to be prepared in several steps. Before you start, remember to read the recipe all the way through. It will give you a good overview. Weigh all the ingredients carefully on your scale, including the liquids!

PARIS BREST

FOR 1 CAKE; SERVES 6
- 300 G (10.6 OZ) CHOUX PASTRY (SEE PASTRY BASICS, P. 27)
- 1 BEATEN EGG
- 20 G (3 TBSP, 0.71 OZ) SLICED ALMONDS

TO GARNISH:
- 200 G (7.1 OZ) GANACHE (SEE PASTRY BASICS, P. 26)
- 150 G (5.3 OZ) CHANTILLY CREAM (SEE PASTRY BASICS, P. 27)
- 350 G (12.3 OZ) PASTRY CREAM (SEE PASTRY BASICS, P. 24)
- 50 G (4 TBSP, 7.76 OZ) PRALINE PASTE (SEE PASTRY BASICS, P. 27)
- 10 G (1 TBSP, 0.35 OZ) ICING SUGAR

Essentially this cake is a large round éclair, filled with generous amounts of delicious praline cream. Originally, Paris-Brest-Paris was a bicycle race. It is said the cake was first made sometime in the early twentieth century to mark this occasion. These days, you can often find it on the menu when the final stage of the Tour de France arrives in Paris.

1. Line a baking tray with baking paper, and preheat the oven to 180°C (350°F).
2. Make the choux pastry. Draw a circle (Ø 20 cm (7.87 in)) with a pencil on your baking paper.
3. Spoon the dough into a piping bag with a large non-serrated nozzle. Pipe choux of about 30 g (1.06 oz) close together all around within the circle. There should be about ten in all.
4. Brush the choux with the egg wash and sprinkle with the sliced almonds.
5. Bake the choux for 35 to 40 minutes. Stick a wooden spatula in between the oven door to allow the steam to escape. Let the cake cool properly before garnishing it.
6. Carefully cut the choux ring in half and place both halves on the work surface. Put the ganache in a piping bag with a non-serrated nozzle, and pipe it all around the base of the cake.
7. Using a whisk, mix the cream, pastry cream and praline into a smooth batter. Fill a piping bag with a large serrated nozzle with the filling, and pipe tall rosettes around the bottom half. Place the top half on the cake, and dust with icing sugar. Slide a cake card under the cake so it does not break.

PEAR TARTE TATIN

FOR 1 CAKE; SERVES 4

- 175 G (6.2 OZ) BUTTER PASTRY (SEE PASTRY BASICS, P. 25)
- 45 G (4 TBSP, 1.59 OZ) GRANULATED SUGAR
- 15 G (1 ½ TBSP, 0.53 OZ) WATER
- 40 G (3 TBSP, 1.41 OZ) UNSALTED BUTTER
- 15 G (1 ½ TBSP, 0.53 OZ) DARK BROWN SUGAR
- 3 CONFERENCE PEARS

Possibly one of the most famous cakes in the world. It is baked upside down, so the butter and sugar at the bottom of the cake tin form a delicious caramelised top layer when the cake is flipped over just before serving (a tarte tatin is eaten warm). The cake was supposedly invented in 1888 by Stéphanie Tatin, who owned a hotel in the Loire Valley with her sister Caroline. One day, she accidentally placed her cake in the oven upside down. And that's how this classic was born.

1. Make the butter pastry the day before so it can stiffen in the refrigerator.
2. Take a round cake tin (Ø 20 cm (7.87 in), 4 cm (1.58 in) high), and a baking tray with a high rim to ensure that any moisture spilling out of your tarte tatin during baking does not spill onto the bottom of your oven. Preheat the oven to 210°C (410°F).
3. Boil the granulated sugar with the water in a saucepan over high heat until a light caramel forms. Add the butter and brown sugar, and keep stirring until everything has nicely dissolved. Pour the mixture into the cake tin, and let it solidify. Please note: the mixture is very hot.
4. Peel the pears. Quarter them, and arrange them with their rounded sides on the caramel.
5. Take the butter pastry from the refrigerator, work it briefly with your hands so it becomes more malleable, and roll it out with the rolling pin into a round sheet the size of the cake tin.
6. Place the dough on the pears, and prick it a few times with a fork.
7. Bake the cake for about 30 minutes at 210°C (410°F).
8. After baking, run a sharp knife along the edges of the tarte tatin to loosen them, and immediately flip it over onto a rack. Beware of the hot juices spilling out of the cake.

> **TIP**
>
> *You can also use apples for this tarte tatin. Choose a sour, firm apple variety. The tart will need to bake a bit longer until the apples are soft, about 50 minutes at 190°C (375°F).*

CHOCOLATE AND DARK CHERRY CAKE

I got the idea for this chocolate and dark cherry cake from Hendrik, a colleague from Ghent. The tart cherries make this chocolate cake irresistibly delicious, with the chocolate cream taking it to the next level.

FOR 1 CAKE; SERVES 8

- 150 G (1 CUP, 5.3 OZ) DRAINED DARK CHERRIES IN SYRUP
- 70 G (5 TBSP, 2.5 OZ) UNSALTED BUTTER, ROOM TEMPERATURE
- 150 G (1 CUP, 5.3 OZ) DARK CHOCOLATE (CHOPPED)
- 100 G (½ CUP, 305 OZ) GRANULATED SUGAR
- 120 G EGG (2 ½ LARGE EGGS, 4.2 OZ)
- 30 G (2 TBSP, 1.06 OZ) SELF-RISING FLOUR (SEE PASTRY BASICS, P. 29)
- ¼ TEASPOON SALT

TO GARNISH:
- 100 G (⅖ CUP, 3.5 OZ) CREAM (40% FAT)
- 65 G (⅖ CUP, 2.3 OZ) DARK CHOCOLATE (CHOPPED)

1. Freeze the drained cherries.
2. Grease a round tart tray (Ø 20 cm (7.87 in), 2.5 cm (1 in) high) with butter, and line it with baking paper. Preheat the oven to 180°C (350°F).
3. Melt the butter in a saucepan, and stir in 150 g (5.3 oz) chocolate (chopped) until completely melted. Set aside to cool.
4. In a large bowl, beat the sugar with the eggs. Make sure not to overbeat it. Otherwise, the batter will rise too much in the oven and then deflate, causing the crust to flake. Add the flour, melted chocolate and salt to the eggs, and mix with a whisk into a smooth batter.
5. Fill the cake tin with the batter, smooth it out, and press the frozen cherries into the batter.
6. Bake the chocolate cake for 30 to 35 minutes. Refrigerate until cool.
7. Put the cream in a saucepan, and bring it to the boil. Remove from the heat, and stir in 65 g of dark chocolate (chopped).
8. Let the mixture cool to body temperature. Spoon the chocolate dressing onto the cake, and spread evenly with a spoon.

GRANDMOTHER'S FLAN CAKE

Everything else pales in comparison once you have eaten this delicious old-fashioned flan cake. I love it.

BASIC RECIPE FOR 1 CAKE OF 6 SERVINGS

- 200 G (7.1 OZ) BUTTER PASTRY (SEE PASTRY BASICS, P. 25)
- 270 G (9.5 OZ) PASTRY CREAM (SEE PASTRY BASICS, P. 24)
- 270 G (1 CUP AND 2 TBSP, 9.5 OZ) WHOLE MILK
- 20 G (2 TBSP, 0.71 OZ) CORNSTARCH
- 20 G (2 TBSP, 0.71 OZ) ALL-PURPOSE FLOUR
- 75 G (5 TBSP, 2.7 OZ) GRANULATED SUGAR
- 5 G (1 TSP, 0.18 OZ) VANILLA SUGAR
- 80 G EGG (1 ½ LARGE EGG, 2.8 OZ)

1. Make the butter pastry an hour in advance so it can stiffen in the fridge.
2. Grease a cake tin (Ø 18 cm (7.08 in), 4 cm (1.58 in) high) with butter. Preheat the oven to 190°C (375°F).
3. Take the pastry from the refrigerator, and work it briefly with your hands so it becomes more malleable. Roll out into a round (Ø 22 cm (8.66 in) and 3 mm (⅛ in thick) on a lightly floured work surface. Line the cake tin with it, and press the sides well so the dough is aligned with the rim of the baking tin. Important: make sure there is no excess dough. Prick the base with a fork.
4. Make the pastry cream.
5. Put the other ingredients in a large measuring cup, and blend until smooth with a hand blender. Add the still warm pastry cream, and continue mixing until you have a smooth batter. You will notice the flan batter is foamy. Sieve it, and pour it into the cake tin.
6. Bake the flan cake for 30 to 60 minutes in a 190°C (375°F) oven.
7. Let the cake cool in the tin for half an hour, after which you can safely remove it. The best way to proceed is as follows: place a round cake card on top of the cake. Make sure it is at least as large as your cake tin. Flip the cake over while pressing down on the cake card with your hand. Carefully remove the cake tin. Place a cake card on top of the cake, and carefully turn it over with both hands.
8. Garnish with chocolate, *brésilienne* or caramel (see below).

> **TIP**
>
> *Make one recipe of the basic pastry-cream recipe. Obviously you will have some left after baking the flan, but this pastry cream is so delicious that it won't sit in your refrigerator for long.*

CHOCOLATE

- 90 G (½ CUP, 3.2 OZ) MILK CHOCOLATE (CHOPPED)
- 50 G (⅕ CUP, 1.76 OZ) CREAM

1. Follow the basic recipe for the traditional flan cake.
2. Melt the chocolate *au bain-marie*, and mix in the cream.
3. Pour onto the cake, and spread it out evenly with a spoon.

BRÉSILIENNE

- 125 G (4.4 OZ) CHANTILLY CREAM (SEE PASTRY BASICS, P. 27)
- 50 G (4 TBSP, 1.76 OZ) *BRÉSILIENNE* NUTS (SEE PASTRY BASICS, P. 25)

1. Follow the basic recipe for the traditional flan cake.
2. Brush the cooled cake with Chantilly cream, and sprinkle with *brésilienne* nuts.

CARAMEL

- 25 G (3 TBSP, 0.88 OZ) WATER
- 80 G (⅖ CUP, 2.8 OZ) GRANULATED SUGAR
- 35 G (2 TBSP, 1.23 OZ) SOFT UNSALTED BUTTER
- 45 G (⅕ CUP, 1.59 OZ) CREAM (40% FAT)

1. Follow the basic recipe for the traditional flan cake.
2. In a heavy-based saucepan, boil the water and sugar until a light caramel forms. Leave the pan on the heat. While stirring, mix the butter into the caramel until melted. The caramel is hot, so protect yourself from splattering. Add the cream while stirring. Continue to stir, then let the sauce cool for a few minutes.
3. Using a spatula, pour the still runny topping over the cake. Spread it out with a spoon. Let cool completely before serving.

SOUTHERN MINI FLAN CAKES

MAKES 5 TARTS

- 340 G (1 ⅖ CUP, 12 OZ) WHOLE MILK
- 165 G (⅘ CUP, 5.8 OZ) GRANULATED SUGAR
- 5 G (1 TSP, 0.18 OZ) CINNAMON
- 35 G (2 ½ TBSP, 1.23 OZ) WHEAT FLOUR
- 3 EGG YOLKS (2.1 OZ)
- 250 G (8.8 OZ) PUFF PASTRY (FRENCH METHOD) (SEE PASTRY BASICS, P. 24)

These mini flan cakes are perfect for summer. The filling is similar to that of Portuguese *pastéis de nata,* but these tarts are baked in a higher tart tin.

1. Boil the milk in a saucepan. Add the granulated sugar, cinnamon and flour, and bring to a boil while stirring. When the filling boils, remove it from the heat, and immediately stir in the egg yolks. Pour the batter into a bowl, cover with cling film, and leave to cool.
2. Grease 5 round mini tart tins (Ø 10 cm (3.93 in) and 2.5 cm (1 in) high) with butter, and preheat the oven to 240°C (460°F).
3. Make the puff pastry, and roll it out to a thickness of 2.5 mm ($\frac{1}{10}$ in). Line the cake tins with it (45 g (1.59 oz) dough per flan cake; there will be some left over). Push up the edges, and prick the base with a fork. Let the dough rest in the tins for an hour. This will prevent it from shrinking during baking.
4. Pour the slightly runny batter into the cake tins (about 110 g (3.9 oz) per flan cake). Use a ladle.
5. Bake for 18 to 20 minutes until dark spots appear on top of the tarts. Let them cool, and then remove them from the cake tin. The flan cakes taste best when still lukewarm.

GOURMAND FLAN CAKE

FOR 2 CAKES; EACH CAKE SERVES 4

- 240 G (8.5 OZ) SHORTBREAD PASTRY (SEE PASTRY BASICS, P. 29)
- 500 G (2 CUPS, 18 OZ) WHOLE MILK
- 100 G (⅖ CUP, 3.5 OZ) CREAM (40% FAT)
- 150 G (¾ CUP, 5.3 OZ) GRANULATED SUGAR
- 8 EGG YOLKS (5.6 OZ)
- 20 G (2 TBSP, 0.71 OZ) VANILLA SUGAR
- 40 G (3 TBSP, 1.41 OZ) CORNSTARCH

Recently, Hendrik, a colleague from Ghent, gave me this flan cake to take home. It was so good, I ate almost all of it, which is why I've included the recipe here.

1. Grease two round cake tins (Ø 14 cm (5.51 in) and 4 cm (1.58 in) high) with butter, and preheat the oven to 180°C (350°F)
2. Remove the shortbread dough from the fridge. Divide into 2 portions of 120 g (4.2 oz) each, and shape into balls. Roll each ball out into a 16 cm (6.30 in) round with the rolling pin, and line the cake tin. Trim any excess dough.
3. Put the rest of the ingredients in a saucepan, and stir well. Bring to a boil while stirring. The batter is ready when it is smooth and there is no foam on top. Pour into a bowl, cover with cling film, and leave to cool.
4. Pour the cooled batter into the cake tins (325 g (11.5 oz) per tin). Smooth with a palette knife.
5. Bake for 40 minutes. Let cool and then remove from the tin. There is no need to garnish your gourmand flan cake.

> **TIP**
>
> *To make a French-style Parisienne flan cake, simply use fluff pastry instead of shortbread pastry. The filling is identical. You can add an extra-sweet finishing touch by spreading sugar syrup on the cake after baking.*

SUMMER FRUIT CAKE

Red fruit makes the summer even sweeter! For this delicious, quick and easy cake, you can use a variety of red summer fruit.

FOR 1 CAKE; SERVES 6

- 200 G (7.1 OZ) SHORTBREAD PASTRY (SEE PASTRY BASICS, P. 29)
- 50 G (1.76 OZ) MILK CHOCOLATE (CHOPPED)
- 450 G (15.87 OZ) PASTRY CREAM (SEE PASTRY BASICS, P. 24)
- 500 G (17.64 OZ) SUMMER FRUIT

TO GARNISH:

- 100 G (3.5 OZ) APRICOT JAM FOR DECORATING (SEE PASTRY BASICS, P. 24)
- 10 G (1 TBSP, 0.35 OZ) ICING SUGAR

1. Lightly grease with butter a rectangular tart tray with removable bottom of 10 × 36 cm (4 × 14.5 in) and 2.5 cm (1 in) high, or a round tart tray with removable bottom (Ø 20 cm (7.87 in) and 2.5 cm (1 in) high). Preheat the oven to 180°C (350°F).
2. Remove the shortbread pastry from the refrigerator. Work it briefly with your hands so it becomes more malleable. Shape into a ball. On a lightly floured work surface, roll out the dough into a Ø 23 cm (9.05 in) round or a 14 × 38 cm (5.52 × 15 in) rectangle, and line the cake tin with it. Trim any excess dough. Press the dough against the edges. Use your thumbs to push the edges up a little. Prick holes in the base with a fork.
3. Blind-bake the cake (see The golden rules of baking, p. 21) for 12 to 15 minutes at 180°C (350°F) until golden. Let cool in the baking tin.
4. Melt the chocolate *au bain-marie*, spread it on the inside of the baked cake, and leave to set. The chocolate keeps the cake nice and crispy.
5. Fill a piping bag with a large non-serrated nozzle with the pastry cream, and pipe pastry cream onto the cake base. Garnish to your liking with fresh fruit, and brush with the glaze.
6. You can dust the edges with icing sugar for a nice finishing touch.

CHEESECAKE

BASIC RECIPE FOR 1 CAKE OF 6 SERVINGS

CAKE BASE:
- 110 G (3.9 OZ) FLEMISH *SPECULOOS* (SEE P. 207)
- 40 G (1.41 OZ) MELTED UNSALTED BUTTER

FILLING:
- 310 G (10.9 OZ) CREAM CHEESE (40% FAT)
- 30 G (2 TBSP, 1.06 OZ) CREAM (40% FAT)
- 110 G (1/2 CUP, 3.9 OZ) GRANULATED SUGAR
- 20 G (2 TBSP, 0.71 OZ) CORNSTARCH
- 30 G (1 ½) EGG YOLK (1.06 OZ)
- 50 G (1 ½) EGG WHITE (1.76 OZ)

This is a delicious authentic recipe from New York. It tastes great, and what's more, it's also easy to make. Slice the cheesecake after it has cooled.

1. Grease a round (Ø 18 cm (7.08 in) and 5 cm (1.97 in) high) springform cake tin with butter, and line it with baking paper.
2. For the cake base, grind the *speculoos* into powder in a food processor. Add the melted butter and mix well. Spread the speculoos mixture around evenly on the bottom of the cake tin. Let the base stiffen in the refrigerator before moving to the next step.
3. For the filling, mix the fresh cheese with the cream, sugar, cornstarch and egg yolk. Beat the egg whites until stiff, and fold them into this mixture with a spatula.

SALTED CARAMEL CHEESECAKE

- 25 G (2 ½ TBSP, 0.88 OZ) WATER
- 80 G (⅖ CUP, 2.8 OZ) GRANULATED SUGAR
- 35 G (2 TBSP, 1.23 OZ) SOFT UNSALTED BUTTER
- 45 G (⅕ CUP, 1.59 OZ) CREAM (40% FAT)
- 1 ½ TSP FLEUR DE SEL
- 50 G (4 TBSP, 1.76 OZ) *BRÉSILIENNE* NUTS (SEE PASTRY BASICS, P. 25)

1. Preheat the oven to 180°C (350°F).
2. Spoon the filling onto the *speculoos* base, and bake the cheesecake for 35 to 40 minutes. Let cool completely before opening the springform and removing the baking paper.
3. In a heavy-based saucepan, boil the water and sugar until a light caramel forms. Leave the pan on the heat. While stirring, mix the butter into the caramel until melted. The filling is hot, so protect yourself from splattering. Add the cream and salt while stirring. Continue to stir, then let the sauce cool for a few minutes.
4. Using a spatula, pour the still runny topping over the cake. Spread it out with a spoon, and decorate with *brésilienne* nuts. Let cool completely before serving.

BLUEBERRY CHEESECAKE

- 150 G (1 ¼ CUP, 5.3 OZ) BLUEBERRIES IN SYRUP, DRAINED (YOU CAN ALSO USE FROZEN BLUEBERRIES)
- 25 G (2 ½ TBSP, 0.88 OZ) GRANULATED SUGAR
- THE JUICE OF ¼ ORANGE
- 25 G (0.88 OZ) FRESH BLUEBERRIES

1. The day before you make your cake, mix 150 g (5.3 oz) of blueberries with the sugar and the juice of ¼ orange. Store in the refrigerator.
2. Before preparing the cake, drain this mixture in a colander. Press the berries with your hands to drain out all the juice. The less juice in the berries, the less the risk of a cake with a soggy bottom.
3. Preheat the oven to 180°C (350°F).
4. Spread the drained blueberries onto the *speculoos* base. Spoon the filling on top of the fruit. Sprinkle fresh blueberries on top of the filling.
5. Bake the cheesecake for 35 to 40 minutes. Let cool completely before opening the springform and removing the baking paper.

TIP

For a plain cheesecake, simply follow the basic recipe. No need for a finishing touch.

WALNUT *CHAGALL*

FOR 1 CAKE; SERVES 6

- 200 G (7.1 OZ) SHORTBREAD PASTRY (SEE PASTRY BASICS, P. 29)
- 120 G (½ CUP, 4.2 OZ) WATER
- 150 G (¾ CUP, 5.3 OZ) DARK BROWN SUGAR
- 50 G (3 ½ TBSP, 1.76 OZ) UNSALTED BUTTER, ROOM TEMPERATURE
- 25 G (2 TBSP, 0.88 OZ) ALL-PURPOSE FLOUR
- A PINCH OF SALT
- 150 G (1 ½ CUP, 5.3 OZ) WALNUT HALVES

This cake is delicious year-round, both in summer and winter. I let it come to room temperature before serving, as the filling stiffens a bit in the refrigerator.

1. Grease a tart tray with removable bottom (Ø 20 cm (7.87 in) and 2.5 cm (1 in) high) with butter. Preheat the oven to 180°C (350°F).
2. Take the shortbread pastry from the refrigerator. Work it briefly with your hands so it becomes more malleable. Shape into a ball. On a lightly floured work surface, roll out the dough into a Ø 23 cm (9.05 in) round, and line the cake tin with it. Trim any excess dough. Press the dough against the edges. Use your thumbs to push the edges up a little. Prick holes in the base with a fork.
3. Blind-bake the cake (see The golden rules of baking, p. 21) for 12 to 15 minutes until golden. Let cool in the baking tin.
4. In a saucepan, boil the water together with the dark brown sugar.
5. Melt the butter in another saucepan. Add the flour. Stir into the butter mixture with a whisk until the mixture starts to bubble.
6. Take both saucepans off the heat. Stir the sugar water into the butter mixture in two batches until smooth.
7. Return the saucepan with the batter to the hob, and allow the mixture to thicken a little more while stirring.
8. Tip in the walnuts. Stir. Then pour the batter onto the baked cake base.
9. Bake the tart for another 10 minutes in a 180°C (350°F) oven. Let cool. Remove from the cake tin.

TIP

Serve the cake with a rosette of Chantilly cream mixed with some raspberries, if you want.

LUXEMBOURGEOISE

FOR 1 CAKE; SERVES 6

- 375 G (13.3 OZ) BUTTER PASTRY (SEE PASTRY BASICS, P. 25)
- 1 BEATEN EGG
- 20 G (3 TBSP, 0.71 OZ) SLICED ALMONDS
- 10 G (1 TBSP, 0.35 OZ) SHINY DECORATING SUGAR

This popular fruit cake from Luxembourg is also a staple in my kitchen. Eat this cake cold. It is a distant relation of the Dutch apple cake, which is filled with apple pieces.

1. Make the butter pastry an hour in advance so it can stiffen in the fridge.
2. Grease a cake tin (Ø 18 cm (7.08 in) and 4 cm (1.58 in) high) with butter. Preheat the oven to 180°C (350°F).
3. Work the dough briefly with your hands until malleable. Divide into two portions, one weighing 225 g (8 oz) and the other 150 g (5.3 oz). Shape each portion into a ball.
4. Roll out the 225 g (8 oz) of dough on a lightly floured work surface into a Ø 22 cm (8.66 in) round that is 3 mm (⅛ in) thick. Line the cake tin with the dough, and press the sides up to the rim of the baking tin. Important: make sure there is no excess dough. Brush the edges with the egg wash, and prick the base with a fork.
5. Fill the cake with a filling of your choice (see below).
6. Roll the rest of the dough into an Ø 18 cm (7.08 in) round and cut it into 2 cm (0.79 in) wide strips. Line up the strips against each other on top of the filling, right up to the rim of the cake tin. When the cake is fully covered, press the edges with your hand.
7. Brush the cake with the egg wash. Sprinkle generously with a mixture of shaved almonds and shiny decorating sugar.
8. Bake for 60 to 70 minutes. Let the cake cool in the cake tin for half an hour. Remove it from the cake tin. The best way to proceed is as follows: place a round cake card on top of the cake. Make sure it is at least as large as your cake tin. Flip the cake over while pressing down on the cake card with your hand. Carefully remove the cake tin. Place another cake card on top of the cake, and carefully turn it over with both hands.

APRICOT AND PINEAPPLE FILLING

- 250 G (8.8 OZ) TINNED PINEAPPLE
- 250 G (8.8 OZ) APRICOTS IN SYRUP
- A MIXTURE OF 15 G (1 TBSP) ALL-PURPOSE FLOUR AND 15 G (1 TBSP) GRANULATED SUGAR

1. Drain the fruit well, chop it into small pieces, and mix it.
2. Sprinkle the flour and sugar mixture on the cake base. Add the fruit.

CHERRY FILLING

- 350 G (2 ½ CUP, 12.3 OZ) DRAINED DARK CHERRIES IN SYRUP
- 150 G (5.3 OZ) PIE SAUCE (SEE PASTRY BASICS, P. 28)

1. Put the cherries in a colander, and drain.
2. Make the pie sauce and mix in the cherries. Let cool before filling the cake.

APPLE AND RAISIN FILLING

- 75 G (½ CUP, 2.7 OZ) RAISINS
- 2 TO 3 APPLES (GOLDEN REINETTE, ELSTAR)
- 25 G (2 TBSP, 0.88 OZ) GRANULATED SUGAR MIXED WITH ¼ TSP CINNAMON

1. Soak the raisins in water for half an hour. Drain in a sieve.
2. Peel the apples, stone them, and cut them into small chunks. Put them in a bowl, and add the raisins along with the sugar and cinnamon.

RHUBARB FILLING

- 350 G (12.3 OZ) RHUBARB
- 150 G (5.3 OZ) PIE SAUCE (SEE PASTRY BASICS, P. 28)
- 10 G (1 TBSP, 0.35 OZ) DARK BROWN SUGAR
- 10 G (1 TBSP, 0.35 OZ) ALL-PURPOSE FLOUR
- A PINCH OF CINNAMON

1. Dice the rhubarb into 1 cm chunks. Make the pie sauce and mix in the rhubarb. Set aside to cool.
2. Sprinkle a mixture of 10 g (1 tbsp, 0.35 oz) of dark brown sugar, 10 g (1 tbsp, 0.35 oz) of flour and a pinch of cinnamon on the cake base, and top with the filling.

PEAR CHARLOTTE CAKE

FOR 1 CAKE; SERVES 4
- 350 G (12.3 OZ) BUTTER PASTRY (SEE PASTRY BASICS, P. 25)
- 1 BEATEN EGG
- 25 G (2 TBSP, 0.88 OZ) JAM TO TASTE
- 4 CONFERENCE PEARS
- 25 G (2 TBSP, 0.88 OZ) DARK BROWN SUGAR
- 15 G (1 TBSP, 0.53 OZ) UNSALTED BUTTER

The best recipes are handed down from generation to generation. This one comes from my old *patron's* recipe collection. Definitely a classic in the making.

1. Grease a round cake ring Ø 18 cm (7.08 in) and 2.5 cm (1 in) high with butter. Line a baking tray with baking paper and preheat the oven to 190°C (375°F).
2. Make the butter pastry, and let it stiffen in the refrigerator.
3. Take the pastry from the refrigerator, and work it briefly with your hands so it becomes more malleable. Divide it into two portions of 175 g (6.1 oz) each, and form them into two rounds.
4. Using a rolling pin, roll out one portion to Ø 22 cm (8.66 in) and a thickness of 3 mm (⅛ in) on a work surface dusted with some flour.
5. Place the cake ring on the baking tray. Line the cake ring with the rolled-out dough. Press the dough up against the sides. Make sure the rim of the dough hangs slightly over the cake tin. Brush the edges with the egg wash. Brush the base with jam.
6. Peel the pears, remove the core, and cut them into 2 cm (0.79 in) cubes. Fill the cake with a pile of cubed pears. Sprinkle the dark brown sugar over the fruit. Arrange 3 knobs of butter on top of the pears.
7. Roll out the second sheet of dough to Ø 20 cm (7.87 in), and drape it over the pears. Using the sides of your hands, press the lid against the rim, and trim any excess dough. Make a Ø 3 cm (1.18 in) hole in the middle of the lid with your finger.
8. Bake for 60 to 70 minutes.

Remove the cake immediately after baking.

TIP

If you like cinnamon, add ¼ teaspoon of cinnamon to the dark brown sugar.

CARAMEL CHOCOLATE FUDGE CAKE

You should definitely try this rich chocolate cake. Caramel chocolate is available in pastilles. The taste is amazing.

FOR 1 CAKE; SERVES 8

- 200 G (7.1 OZ) SHORTBREAD PASTRY (SEE PASTRY BASICS, P. 29)

FOR THE FUDGE FILLING:

- 150 G (⅘ CUP, 5.3 OZ) CARAMEL CHOCOLATE (CHOPPED)
- 50 G (⅖ CUP, 1.76 OZ) MILK CHOCOLATE (CHOPPED)
- 100 G (⅖ CUP, 3.5 OZ) CREAM (40% FAT)
- 50 G (⅓ CUP, 1.76 OZ) ROASTED HAZELNUTS (SEE PASTRY BASICS, P. 26), CHOPPED

TO GARNISH:

- 50 G (⅖ CUP, 1.76 OZ) CARAMEL CHOCOLATE (CHOPPED)
- 50 G (⅖ CUP, 1.76 OZ) DARK CHOCOLATE (CHOPPED)
- 50 G (3 TBSP, 1.76 OZ) UNSALTED BUTTER, ROOM TEMPERATURE
- 50 G (⅕ CUP, 1.76 OZ) CREAM (40% FAT)
- 50 G (⅓ CUP, 1.76 OZ) WHOLE ROASTED HAZELNUTS (SEE PASTRY BASICS, P. 26)

1. Grease a round tart tray with removable bottom (Ø 20 cm (7.87 in) and 2.5 cm (1 in) high) with butter. Preheat the oven to 180°C (350°F).
2. Take the shortbread pastry from the refrigerator, and work it briefly with your hands so it becomes more malleable. On a lightly floured work surface, roll out the dough into a Ø 23 cm (9.05 in) round, and line the baking tin with it. Press the dough against the edges. Make sure there is no excess dough. Use your thumbs to push the edges up a little. Prick the base with a fork.
3. Blind-bake the cake (see The golden rules of baking, p. 21) for 12 to 15 minutes until golden. Let cool and remove from the cake tin.
4. For the fudge filling, melt the caramel chocolate and the milk chocolate *au bain-marie*. Once melted, stir in the cream and nuts.
5. Pour the filling into the base, and spread out the batter evenly with a spoon. Leave to cool (may be refrigerated).
6. For the finishing touch, melt the caramel chocolate, the dark chocolate and the butter *au bain-marie*. Stir in the cream.
7. Immediately pour the mixture over the cake, and smooth it out evenly with a spoon to the edges. Decorate with some hazelnuts.

TIP

If you love salted caramel, use salted butter.

ÉCLAIR *PARISIEN*

Hosting a party? Éclairs are a fun alternative to a traditional cake. Be sure to make enough of these moreish éclairs, though!

MAKES 8 ÉCLAIRS

- 1 RECIPE CHOUX PASTRY (SEE PASTRY BASICS, P. 27)
- 600 G (21 OZ) PASTRY CREAM (SEE PASTRY BASICS, P. 24)

TO GARNISH:
- 100 G (⅖ CUP, 3.5 OZ) CREAM (40% FAT)
- 150 G (⅗ CUP, 5.3 OZ) DARK CHOCOLATE (CHOPPED)
- 100 G (½ CUP, 3.5 OZ) CHOCOLATE FLAKES

1. Line a baking tray with baking paper, and preheat the oven to 180°C (350°F).
2. Make the choux pastry according to the basic recipe.
3. Fill a piping bag with a medium-sized serrated nozzle with the choux pastry. Pipe 8 long strips, each about 15 cm (5.90 in) long and weighing some 50 g (1.76 oz).
4. Bake for 30 to 35 minutes. Stick a wooden spatula between the oven door so it is ajar. This allows the vapour to escape, preventing the pastry from deflating. Set aside to cool.
5. Pierce three holes in the bottom of each éclair and fill it with pastry cream (75 g (2.7 oz) per éclair). Use a piping bag with a small non-serrated nozzle.
6. In a saucepan, bring 100 g (3.5 oz) of cream to a boil. Remove the pan from the heat, and stir in the chopped dark chocolate until fully melted. Let the mixture cool to body temperature.
7. Press the top of the éclairs into the chocolate, and wipe off any excess chocolate with your finger. Press both ends into the chocolate flakes.

TEA PIE WITH A SWEET FRUIT FILLING

MAKES 5 SMALL PIES

- 250 G (1 ½ CUP, 8.8 OZ) FROZEN BLUEBERRIES
- 300 G (10.6 OZ) BUTTER PASTRY (SEE PASTRY BASICS, P. 25)
- 125 G (4.4 OZ) PIE SAUCE (SEE PASTRY BASICS, P. 28)

These pies are incredibly tasty. I went with a blueberry filling in this instance, but other fillings are equally delicious (see Delicious fruit pies, p. 165). These pies should be eaten almost straight out of the oven, when the dough is still crispy. They are a variation on the Antwerp plum tarts.

1. Put the blueberries in a colander, and let them thaw and drain.
2. Make the butter pastry an hour in advance, allowing it to stiffen in the refrigerator.
3. Add 125 g (4.4 oz) of warm pie sauce to the blueberries, mix, and leave to cool.
4. Grease 5 mini tart tins Ø 10 cm (3.93 in) and 2.5 cm (1 in) high with butter, and preheat the oven to 200°C (400°F).
5. Take the butter pastry from the refrigerator, and work it briefly with your hands so it becomes more malleable. Using a rolling pin, roll out two-thirds of the dough on a lightly floured work surface to a thickness of 3 mm (⅛ in). Cut out 12 cm (4.72 in) rounds, and line the tart tins with them. Prick the base several times with a fork.
6. Fill the pies with the fruit filling (75 g (2.7 oz) per serving).
7. Roll out the rest of the dough into a 2 mm (1/12 in) thick rectangle. Cut it into 2 cm (0.79 in) wide strips with a pastry wheel. Make a lattice pie crust with the strips for each of the pies.
8. Place the tart tins on a baking tray and bake for 20 minutes until golden brown.

ON THE CAKE STAND

MAKES 6 TARTS

CAKE BASE:

- 300 G (10.6 OZ) SHORTBREAD PASTRY (SEE PASTRY BASICS, P. 29)
- 225 G (1 CUP, 8 OZ) PURE LEMON JUICE
- 140 G (⅗ CUP, 4.9 OZ) WATER
- 180 G (1 CUP, 6.3 OZ) GRANULATED SUGAR
- 30 G (3 TBSP, 1.06 OZ) CORNSTARCH
- 2 EGG YOLKS (1.41 OZ)
- 10 G (2 TSP, 0.35 OZ) LEMON ZEST
- 70 G (5 TBSP, 2.5 OZ) UNSALTED BUTTER, ROOM TEMPERATURE

TO GARNISH:

- 400 G (14.1 OZ) MERINGUE BATTER (HOT OR COLD PREPARATION OF YOUR CHOICE, SEE PASTRY BASICS, P. 27)

CITRONELLA

I always decorate my lemon tarts with meringue. The sour lemon filling and sweet meringue complement each other beautifully.

1. Grease 6 mini tart tins (Ø 10 cm (3.93 in), 2.5 cm (1 in) high) with butter, and preheat the oven to 180°C (350°F).
2. Take the shortbread pastry from the refrigerator, and work it briefly with your hands so it becomes more malleable. Weigh out 6 portions of 50 g (1.76 oz) each, and shape them into balls. On a lightly floured work surface, roll out the balls into 12 cm (5.72 in) discs, and line the tart tins with the dough. Press the dough against the sides. Make sure you don't have any excess dough.
3. Blind-bake the tarts (see The golden rules of baking, p. 21) for 12 to 15 minutes until golden. Let them cool in the tin. Remove them from the tin.
4. For the filling, put all the ingredients except the butter in a saucepan, and mix well. Bring to the boil while stirring. The batter is ready when it is smooth and sufficiently bound. Remove from the heat, and mix in the butter with a hand blender.
5. Immediately fill the tart tins with the batter (80 g (2.8 oz) per tart), and leave to cool.
6. Fill a piping bag with a large non-serrated nozzle with the meringue batter, and pipe a thick mound onto the lemon batter (60 g (2.1 oz) per tart).
7. Pop the tart under a hot grill for about three minutes, or use a culinary torch to caramelise it.

> **TIP**
>
> *For a fruit tart, you can also fill the blind-baked tarts with Swiss cream (see Pastry basics, p. 29) (75 g (2.7 oz) per tart) and garnish it with fresh fruit.*

MAKES 8 CHOUQUETTES

- 400 G (14.1 OZ) SHORTBREAD PASTRY (SEE PASTRY BASICS, P. 29)
- 1 RECIPE CHOUX PASTRY (SEE PASTRY BASICS, P. 27)
- 50 G (4 TBSP, 1.76 OZ) SHINY DECORATING SUGAR

TO GARNISH:

- 600 G (21 OZ) CHANTILLY CREAM (SEE PASTRY BASICS, P. 27)
- 24 RASPBERRIES

CHOUQUETTE

These stunning top-hat tarts should be served cold. They can be kept in the refrigerator for about three days and are incredibly delicious.

1. Grease 8 non-serrated mini tart tins (Ø 9 cm (3.54 in), 1.5 cm (0.60 in) high) with butter. Preheat the oven to 180°C (350°C).
2. Take the shortbread pastry from the refrigerator, and work it briefly with your hands so it becomes more malleable. Using a rolling pin, roll it out until 3 mm (⅛ in) thick on a lightly floured work surface. Cut out rounds (Ø 12 cm (4.72 in), about 50 g (1.76 oz) of dough per round). Line the mini tart tins with the dough rounds. Prick the base with a fork.
3. Make the choux batter.
4. Fill a piping bag with a large, non-serrated nozzle with the batter, and pipe a chou onto the base (50 g (1.76 oz) per choux tart). Sprinkle the choux tart with shiny decorating sugar.
5. Bake for 30-35 minutes. Stick a wooden spatula between the oven door so it is ajar. This allows the steam to escape, preventing the pastry from deflating. Set aside to cool.
6. Using a sharp knife, cut the lid off the tarts.
7. Fill a piping bag with a serrated nozzle with the Chantilly cream. Pipe cream into the cavity, and press three raspberries into the cream. Garnish the tarts with a rosette of Chantilly cream, and place the lid back on top of the chouquette.

TARTELETTE MAISON

FOR 4 TARTLETS

- 125 G (4.2 OZ) PIE SAUCE (SEE PASTRY BASICS, P. 28)
- 250 G (1 ⅔ CUP, 8.8 OZ) DRAINED DARK CHERRIES IN SYRUP
- 200 G (7.1 OZ) CHOUX PASTRY (SEE PASTRY BASICS, P. 27)
- 50 G (3 TBSP, 1.76 OZ) PASTRY CREAM (SEE PASTRY BASICS, P. 24)
- 200 G (7.1 OZ) (FRENCH-STYLE) PUFF PASTRY (SEE PASTRY BASICS, P. 24)
- 30 G (4 TBSP, 1.06 OZ) SLICED ALMONDS
- 300 G (10.6 OZ) CHANTILLY CREAM (SEE PASTRY BASICS, P. 27)
- 5 G (1 TBSP, 0.18 OZ) ICING SUGAR
- 4 BIGARREAU CHERRY HALVES

A cherry and Chantilly cream tartlet on a choux pastry base. Like so many 'typically French' specialities, this dough was invented by a foreigner. In 1540, signore Popelini, the chef of the French queen Catherine de' Medici, created *pâte à chaud*, a cake that was dried over a fire so the water would evaporate. The name was later bastardised into *pâte à choux*.

1. Make your pie sauce first, add the drained cherries, and leave to cool.
2. Grease 4 mini tart tins Ø 10 cm (3.93 in) and 2.5 cm (1 in) high with butter. Preheat the oven to 200°C (400°F).
3. Make the choux pastry dough, and mix in the pastry cream.
4. Prepare the puff pastry, roll it out to 2.5 mm (¹⁄₁₀ in) thickness, and line the tart tins with it. You need about 45 g (1.59 oz) of dough per tart (you will have some leftovers). Prick the base with a fork. Fill the moulds with the batter, and smooth it out nicely.
5. Sprinkle the shaved almonds over the batter.
6. Bake the tartlets for 20 to 25 minutes.
7. Immediately after baking, carefully cut the tops off the tartlets with a serrated knife. Carefully remove the lids with a wide palette knife, and place them upside down on a wire rack. Using a spoon, remove any remaining batter on the lid and the tart base. Be careful, they are piping hot!
8. After cooling, spread the cherries on the tart base. Pipe Chantilly cream rosettes around the edge of the tartlet. Also pipe some Chantilly cream in the centre of the tartlet.
9. Put the lid back on the tartlet. Dust with icing sugar. Pipe a rosette of whipped cream onto the centre of the lid, and garnish with half a Bigarreau cherry.

MAKES 5 TARTLETS

- 200 G (7.1 OZ) SHORTBREAD PASTRY (SEE PASTRY BASICS, P. 29)
- 375 G (13.2 OZ) WALNUT PASTE (SEE PASTRY BASICS, P. 29)
- 100 G (1 CUP, 3.5 OZ) PECANS

TO GARNISH:

- 40 G (1.41 OZ) CREAM CHEESE
- 100 G (⅔ CUP, 3.5 OZ) ICING SUGAR
- 5 EXTRA PECANS

NUT TARTLET

This soft tartlet is very easy to make. A great-tasting, moreish treat! Perfect as a snack or when you are peckish.

1. Grease 5 mini tart tins (Ø 10 cm (3.93 in), 2.5 cm (1 in) high) with butter, and preheat the oven to 200°C (400°F).
2. Make the shortbread pastry at least 1 hour in advance so it can stiffen in the refrigerator.
3. Divide the dough into 5 portions of 40 g (1.41 oz) each, and shape into balls. Using a rolling pin, roll out the balls into round 12 cm (5.72 in) discs, and line the tart tins with the dough. Prick a few holes in the base with a fork.
4. Fill the moulds evenly with the walnut paste, and garnish with pecans.
5. Place the tart tins on a baking tray. Bake for 20 to 25 minutes, and leave to cool.
6. While stirring, melt the fresh cheese in a pan over low heat. Add the icing sugar, and continue to stir until a liquid glaze forms. This takes very little time. Make sure the mixture does not get hot.
7. Brush the cakes with the glaze, garnish with a pecan, and leave to set.

THE TASTIEST CARROT CAKE

FOR 1 CAKE; SERVES 12

- 300 G (10.6 OZ) BUTTER PASTRY (SEE PASTRY BASICS, P. 25)
- 150 G (5.3 OZ) APRICOT JAM (SEE PASTRY BASICS, P. 24)
- 150 G (1 CUP, 5.3 OZ) SELF-RISING FLOUR (SEE PASTRY BASICS, P. 29)
- 165 G (¾ CUP, 5.8 OZ) GRANULATED SUGAR
- 150 G (5.3 OZ) SUNFLOWER OIL
- 2 ½ EGG (4.6 OZ)
- ½ TSP CINNAMON
- 1 TSP LEMON ZEST
- A PINCH OF SALT
- 150 G (5.3 OZ) FINELY GRATED CARROTS
- 75 G (⅔ CUP, 2.7 OZ) ROASTED HAZELNUTS (SEE PASTRY BASICS, P. 26), CHOPPED

TO GARNISH:

- 200 G (7.1 OZ) PHILADELPHIA CREAM CHEESE
- 100 G (¾ CUP, 3.5 OZ) ICING SUGAR
- 150 G (5.3 OZ) UNSALTED BUTTER, ROOM TEMPERATURE
- 50 G (¼ CUP, 1.76 OZ) ROASTED HAZELNUTS (SEE PASTRY BASICS, P. 26), CHOPPED

I got this recipe from a Moroccan chef on one of my surfing trips, and it is absolutely the best carrot cake I have ever made and tasted.

1. Make the shortbread pastry at least 2 hours in advance so it can stiffen in the refrigerator.
2. Lightly grease a 20 × 20 cm (7.87 × 7.87 in) and 4 cm (1.58 in) high baking tin with softened butter. Line it with baking paper. Preheat the oven to 180°C (350°F).
3. Work the dough briefly with your hands so it becomes more malleable. Roll it out into a 26 cm (10.23 in) square. Line the cake tin with it. Press the sides well, and prick the base with a fork. Spread a thin layer of apricot jam on the bottom.
4. Put the flour, sugar, oil, eggs, cinnamon, lemon and pinch of salt in a bowl. Stir vigorously with a spatula for a few minutes. Stir in the carrots and nuts.
5. Tip the filling into the baking tin, and bake the cake for 35 to 40 minutes. Leave to cool completely.
6. Put the cheese and the icing sugar in a bowl, and whisk until smooth. Beat the butter until fluffy, and add it. Mix. Spoon the frosting onto the cake, spreading it evenly. Decorate with the chopped hazelnuts.

BUDINI DI RISO

MAKES 10 TARTS

- 1000 G (4 CUPS, 35.2 OZ) WHOLE MILK
- 150 G (¾ CUP, 5.3 OZ) RISOTTO (OR DESSERT) RICE
- 125 G (⅗ CUP, 4.4 OZ) GRANULATED SUGAR
- 200 G (7.1 OZ) PASTRY CREAM (SEE PASTRY BASICS, P. 24)
- 1 EGG
- 10 G (2 TSP, 0.35 OZ) LEMON ZEST
- 400 G (14.1 OZ) BUTTER PASTRY (SEE PASTRY BASICS, P. 25)

TO GARNISH:

- 10 G (1 TBSP, 0.35 OZ) ICING SUGAR

Walk past any authentic *pasticceria* in Florence, and you will see these cakes in their window. A breakfast staple, they also taste great as a snack or even as a dessert (with a scoop of ice cream and some fresh summer fruit).

1. Grease 10 muffin tins (Ø 8 cm (3.15 in) and 4 cm (1.58 in) high) with butter, and preheat the oven to 200°C (400°F).
2. Put the milk in a heavy-bottom saucepan, and bring it to a boil. Stir in the rice. Put the lid on the pot, and let the rice pudding simmer on low heat for half an hour or a little longer, until the rice has absorbed almost all the milk. Stir occasionally to prevent the rice pudding from sticking to the sides.
3. Remove the rice pudding from the heat, and spoon it into a bowl. Stir in the sugar, and leave to cool.
4. Using a spatula, gently fold the pastry cream into the rice along with the egg and grated lemon zest. You want the rice to retain its shape.
5. Take the shortbread pastry from the refrigerator, and work it briefly with your hands so it becomes more malleable. Divide into 10 balls, each weighing 40 g (1.41 oz).
6. Using the rolling pin, roll out the dough on a lightly floured work surface into rounds (Ø 10 cm (3.93 in) and 2.5-3 mm (1/8 in) thick). Line the baking tins with the dough. Make sure there is as little excess dough as possible. Push up the edges of the dough with your thumbs, and prick the base with a fork.
7. Fill a piping bag with a large nozzle, pipe the rice filling into the base, and bake for about 30 minutes. Dust with icing sugar for a nice finishing touch.

DELICIOUS FRUIT PIES

These ten fruit pies will leave you wanting more. They are so delicious! They are also quick and easy to make, which is always handy when you are short on time. Taste the bounty of nature and all the delicious things it has to offer in every bite. In late summer, head into the forest with your pail to pick blueberries and other wild berries at picking sites. Self-picking farms and gardens are also worth investigating, as they often have even more of a selection. Mix the berries with some sugar water and store them in the freezer for when you feel like making one of these fruit pies. A burst of summer sweetness for your taste buds!

APPLE PIE *ALSACIENNE*

FOR 1 PIE; SERVES 4
- 3 FIRM SOUR APPLES
- 100 G (⅖ CUP, 3.5 OZ) CREAM (40% FAT)
- 1 EGG YOLK (0.71 OZ)
- 50 G (⅖ CUP, 1.76 OZ) ICING SUGAR
- 20 G (2 TBSP, 0.71 OZ) ALL-PURPOSE FLOUR
- 1 *VLAAI* PIE CRUST (SEE PASTRY BASICS, P. 28)

I never turn down a slice of this apple pie. Unlike other apple pies, this one is filled with a custard-like mixture of egg, sugar, flour and cream. This pie is especially famous in Alsace (France).

1. Preheat the oven to 200°C (400°F).
2. Peel the apples, core them, and then cut them into four pieces.
3. Put the cream, egg yolk, sugar and flour in a small bowl, and mix well.
4. Arrange the apple pieces on the pie base. Pour the sauce over the apples.
5. Let the pie rise for another 15 minutes. Bake for 45 minutes.

TIP

You can add some kirsch (sour cherry liqueur) to the sauce.

FOR 1 PIE; SERVES 4

- 125 G (4.4 OZ) PIE SAUCE (SEE PASTRY BASICS, P. 28)
- 300 G (2 ⅖ CUPS, 10.6 OZ) DRAINED DARK CHERRIES IN SYRUP
- 5 G (1 TBSP, 0.18 OZ) ICING SUGAR
- 1 (VEGAN) *VLAAI* PIE CRUST (SEE PASTRY BASICS, P. 28)

CHERRY PIE (VEGAN)

Did you know that cherries belong to the plum family? For this pie, I prefer to use dark cherries instead of the sweeter red ones: the combination of the tart cherries and the sweet pie sauce is delicious.

1. Preheat the oven to 200°C (400°F).
2. Put the cherries in a colander, and drain. Make the pie sauce and mix in the cherries. Set aside to cool.
3. Spread the cherry filling over the pie base. Let rise for another 15 minutes.
4. Bake the pie for 25 to 30 minutes.
5. Let the pie cool, and dust the edges with icing sugar.

OLD-FASHIONED APPLE PIE

FOR 1 PIE; SERVES 4

- DOUBLE PIE-DOUGH RECIPE DIVIDED INTO TWO PORTIONS OF 200 G
- 400 G (4.1 OZ) EXTRA-DRY APPLE SAUCE WITH PIECES
- 1 BEATEN EGG
- 50 G (¼ CUP, 1.76 OZ) SHINY DECORATING SUGAR
- 1 *VLAAI* PIE CRUST (SEE PASTRY BASICS, P. 28)

I like this popular pie best with apple sauce made from sour apples. The sugar on the lid adds a nice crunch. This pie can be served hot or cold.

1. Preheat the oven to 200°C (400°F).
2. Spread the apple sauce on the pie base.
3. Roll out the second 200 g (7.1 oz) piece of dough Ø 22 cm (8.66 in). Fold it into four, and cut out a pie lid. Fold it open again.
4. Cover the apple sauce with the dough, and pinch the edges. Brush the dough with the egg wash, and dust it with the decorating sugar. Let rise for another 15 minutes.
5. Bake the pie for 25 to 30 minutes.

TIP

For a closed vegan apple pie, use the vegan vlaai *pie crust for the lid (see Pastry basics, p. 28), and substitute the beaten egg with water.*

Sprinkle a teaspoon of cinnamon on the applesauce for an even more flavourful tart.

PLUM PIE (VEGAN)

FOR 1 PIE; SERVES 4

- 400 G (14.1 OZ) RIPE PLUMS (BLUE REINE VICTORIA OR GREEN REINE CLAUDE)
- 10 G (1 TBSP, 0.35 OZ) GRANULATED SUGAR
- 10 G (1 TBSP, 0.35 OZ) ALL-PURPOSE FLOUR
- A PINCH OF CINNAMON
- 20 G (2 TBSP, 0.71 OZ) GRANULATED SUGAR
- 1 (VEGAN) *VLAAI* PIE CRUST (SEE PASTRY BASICS, P. 28)

This pie is made with fresh, ripe plums. Add a nice finishing touch with some granulated sugar!

1. Preheat the oven to 200°C (400°F).
2. Halve the plums and remove the stones.
3. Mix 10 g (1 tbsp, 0.35 oz) of sugar with 10 g (1 tbsp, 0.35 oz) of flour, and season with a pinch of cinnamon. Sprinkle the sugar mixture over the base. This prevents the moisture from the plums from seeping into the pie base. No soggy bottoms!
4. Score each half of the soft plums twice with a knife, plunging the blade in two-thirds of the way. Line the tin with the plums, with the scored side facing up. Let rise for another 15 minutes.
5. Bake the pie for 30 to 35 minutes at 200°C (400°F). After baking, sprinkle generously with the 20 g of granulated sugar.

GOOSEBERRY PIE (VEGAN)

FOR 1 PIE, SERVES 4

- 300 G (10.6 OZ) DRAINED GOOSEBERRIES IN SYRUP
- 125 G (4.4 OZ) PIE SAUCE (SEE PASTRY BASICS, P. 28)
- 10 G (1 TBSP, 0.35 OZ) GRANULATED SUGAR
- 10 G (1 TBSP, 0.35 OZ) ALL-PURPOSE FLOUR
- A PINCH OF CINNAMON
- 5 G (1 TBSP, 0.18 OZ) ICING SUGAR
- 1 (VEGAN) *VLAAI* PIE CRUST (SEE PASTRY BASICS, P. 28)

Gooseberries are easy to grow yourself. These berry bushes do not require full sun; a little shade is ideal. The flavours range from sour to sweet.

1. Preheat the oven to 200°C (400°F).
2. Put the gooseberries in a colander, and drain. Make the pie sauce and mix in the berries. Set aside to cool.
3. Sprinkle the pie base with a mixture of 10 g (1 tbsp, 0.35 oz) of granulated sugar, 10 g (1 tbsp, 0.35 oz) of flour and a pinch of cinnamon. Spread the gooseberry filling over the pie base, and leave to rise for another 15 minutes.
4. Bake the pie for 30 to 35 minutes.
5. Let the pie cool, and dust the edges with icing sugar.

FOR 1 PIE; SERVES 4

- 300 G (10.6 OZ) FROZEN BLUEBERRIES
- 125 G (4.4 OZ) PIE SAUCE (SEE PASTRY BASICS, P. 28)
- 100 G (3.5 OZ) OAT FLAKE CRUMBLE (VEGAN) (SEE PASTRY BASICS, P. 26)
- 1 (VEGAN) *VLAAI* PIE CRUST (SEE PASTRY BASICS, P. 28)

BLUEBERRY PIE WITH AN OAT FLAKE CRUMBLE TOPPING (VEGAN)

This pie is delicious in the morning. The healthy crumble topping makes this a great breakfast staple.

1. Preheat the oven to 200°C (400°F).
2. Tip the frozen fruit into a colander, let it thaw, and drain the liquid.
3. Make the pie sauce, and mix in the blueberries. Set aside to cool.
4. Spread the blueberry filling over the pie base, and sprinkle generously with the oat-flake crumble. Let rise for another 15 minutes.
5. Bake the pie for 30 to 35 minutes.

TIP

For a vegan pie, substitute the butter with margarine in the crumble.

DELICIOUS FRUIT PIES

RHUBARB PIE (VEGAN)

FOR 1 PIE; SERVES 4

- 125 G (4.4 OZ) PIE SAUCE (SEE PASTRY BASICS, P. 28)
- 300 G (10.6 OZ) RHUBARB
- 10 G (1 TBSP, 0.35 OZ) DARK BROWN SUGAR
- 10 G (1 TBSP, 0.35 OZ) ALL-PURPOSE FLOUR
- A PINCH OF CINNAMON
- 100 G (3.5 OZ) BUTTER CRUMBLE (VEGAN) (SEE PASTRY BASICS, P. 25)
- 5 G (1 TBSP, 0.18 OZ) ICING SUGAR
- 1 (VEGAN) *VLAAI* PIE CRUST (SEE PASTRY BASICS, P. 28)

This delicious rhubarb pie is easy to make and incredibly delicious. The fresh tart rhubarb combines beautifully with the sweet crumble.

1. Preheat the oven to 200°C (400°F).
2. Dice the rhubarb into chunks of 1 cm (0.39 in). Make the pie sauce, and mix in the rhubarb. Set aside to cool.
3. Sprinkle a mixture of 10 g (1 tbsp, 0.35 oz) of dark brown sugar, 10 g (1 tbsp, 0.35 oz) of flour and a pinch of cinnamon over the pie base.
4. Spread the rhubarb filling over the pie base. Sprinkle with the crumble. Let rise for another 15 minutes.
5. Bake the pie for 30 to 35 minutes.
6. Let cool, and dust the edges with icing sugar if necessary.

TIP

You can also top the filling with some sliced strawberries before baking. For a vegan pie, substitute the butter in the crumble with margarine.

FOR 1 PIE; SERVES 4

- 300 G (10.6 OZ) FROZEN FOREST FRUITS
- 125 G (4.4 OZ) PIE SAUCE (SEE PASTRY BASICS, P. 28)
- 1 (VEGAN) *VLAAI* PIE CRUST (SEE PASTRY BASICS, P. 28)

FOREST FRUIT PIE (VEGAN)

Did you know that frozen fruit is just as healthy and delicious as fresh fruit? Mixed frozen forest fruit is ideal for use in pastries. Frozen fruit should always be thawed first and drained well, otherwise the pastry will be too watery.

1. Preheat the oven to 200°C (400°F).
2. Tip the frozen fruit into a colander, let it thaw, and drain the liquid.
3. Make the pie sauce, and mix in the forest fruits. Set aside to cool.
4. Spread the forest fruit filling over the base. Let rise for another 15 minutes.
5. Bake the pie for 30 to 35 minutes.

APRICOT PIE
(VEGAN)

This classic apricot pie is made from tinned apricot halves so you can bake it year-round. The cake tastes even better thanks to the apricot glaze, which is added after baking.

> **FOR 1 PIE; SERVES 4**
> - 300 G (10.6 OZ) APRICOT HALVES IN SYRUP
> - 10 G (1 TBSP, 0.35 OZ) GRANULATED SUGAR
> - 10 G (1 TBSP, 0.35 OZ) ALL-PURPOSE FLOUR
> - 100 G (3.5 OZ) APRICOT JAM FOR DECORATING (SEE PASTRY BASICS, P. 24)
> - 1 (VEGAN) *VLAAI* PIE CRUST (SEE PASTRY BASICS, P. 28)

1. Preheat the oven to 200°C (400°F).
2. Put the apricots in a colander, and drain.
3. Sprinkle a mixture of 10 g (1 tbsp, 0.35 oz) of sugar and 10 g (1 tbsp, 0.35 oz) of flour over the pie base. Arrange the apricots on top of the filling as shown in the photo. Let rise for another 15 minutes.
4. Bake the pie for 30 to 35 minutes.
5. After baking, generously brush the cake with the apricot glaze.

FOR 1 PIE; SERVES 4

- 250 G (1 CUP, 8.8 OZ) PASTRY CREAM (SEE PASTRY BASICS, P. 24)
- 7 APRICOT HALVES IN SYRUP
- 200 G (7.1 OZ) TINNED PINEAPPLE CHUNKS IN SYRUP
- 1 APPLE (BOSKOOP, BRAMLEY, GRANNY SMITH)
- 50 G (1.76 OZ) APRICOT JAM FOR DECORATING (SEE PASTRY BASICS, P. 24)
- 1 *VLAAI* PIE CRUST (SEE PASTRY BASICS, P. 28)

PANANE PIE

This *panane* pie is a special tart originating from the French Alsace region. The name is a blend of French *pomme* (apple) and *ananas* (pineapple), two delicious fruits to combine. I like to make this pie with apples, apricots and pineapple. You can also use peaches or plums.

1. Preheat the oven to 200°C (400°F).
2. Using a piping bag with a non-serrated nozzle, pipe a layer of pastry cream onto the base. Decorate the pastry cream with the fruits as shown. Let rise for another 15 minutes.
3. Bake the pie for 30 to 35 minutes.
4. After baking, brush with the apricot glaze.

WAFFLE FEST

There are many different types of waffles, each made in a different way and each with its own specific flavour and texture. But nothing beats sitting around the table and tucking into a freshly baked waffle with friends or family. One recipe that I reckon most people will love is chocolate-dipped Liège waffles. Deliciously rich in flavour, not dry, and just as tasty a few days after baking. I started experimenting with my heart-shaped waffle maker and ended up with five different waffles, from filled *kermishartjes* to vegan heart-shaped waffles. The tastiest waffles are those you make yourself, with the fragrance of butter, vanilla, cinnamon and love filling your kitchen.

HEART-SHAPED WAFFLES

Besides tasting amazing, these heart-shaped waffles also look gorgeous. You can choose between all kinds of hearts. Crispy, fluffy, filled, *speculoos*, vegan, chocolate…

HEART-SHAPED FUNFAIR WAFFLES

FOR 15 WAFFLES

- 25 G (0.88 OZ) FRESH YEAST OR 1 TBSP (0.32 OZ) INSTANT DRY YEAST
- 45 G (⅕ CUP, 1.59 OZ) WHOLE MILK
- 190 G (1 ½ CUP, 6.7 OZ) ALL-PURPOSE FLOUR
- 75 G (5 TBSP, 2.5 OZ) UNSALTED BUTTER, ROOM TEMPERATURE
- 1 SMALL (1.41 OZ) EGG
- 10 G (1 TBSP, 0.35 OZ) GRANULATED SUGAR
- A PINCH OF SALT
- FILLING OF YOUR CHOICE
- ICING SUGAR

FILLING FOR 15 DARK BROWN SUGAR WAFFLES

- 270 G (9.5 OZ) BUTTER
- 100 G (⅔ CUP, 3.5 OZ) ICING SUGAR
- 120 G (½ CUP, 4.2 OZ) DARK BROWN SUGAR
- 15 G (1 ½ TBSP, 0.53 OZ) WATER
- ½ TEASPOON CINNAMON

FILLING FOR 15 VANILLA WAFFLES

- 250 G (8.8 OZ) BUTTER
- 200 G (1 ½ CUP, 7.1 OZ) ICING SUGAR
- 25 G (3 TBSP, 0.88 OZ) WATER
- 15 G (3 TSP, 0.53 OZ) VANILLA SUGAR

1. Put the yeast in a bowl (if dry yeast, crumble it). Add the milk, flour, butter, egg, sugar and salt, and mix to form a homogeneous mass. Knead on your work surface for five minutes.
2. Weigh out 15 portions of 25 g (0.88 oz) each, and shape into balls. Let the dough rest under a towel for an hour.
3. Preheat the waffle maker on medium. Lightly brush with softened butter.
4. Place a dough ball on each heart. Close the waffle maker, and keep pressing it down for about 1 minute until the waffle is baked.
5. Take the waffles out of the waffle maker one by one, immediately cut them in half with a sharp serrated blade (remember: they are hot!), and let them cool.
6. Spread the filling of your choice on one half of the waffles, and place the other half on top to form a waffle sandwich. You need about 30 g of filling per waffle. Dust with icing sugar.

Filling for 15 dark brown sugar waffles:
Beat the butter until fluffy, and mix in the icing sugar, dark brown sugar, water and ½ teaspoon of cinnamon.

Filling for 15 vanilla waffles:
Beat the butter until fluffy, and mix in the icing sugar, water and vanilla sugar.

CRISPY HEART-SHAPED WAFFLES

FOR 25 WAFFLES

- 150 G (1 CUP, 5.3 OZ) SELF-RISING FLOUR (SEE PASTRY BASICS, P. 29)
- 120 G (½ CUP, 4.2 OZ) WHOLE MILK
- 120 G (½ CUP, 4.2 OZ) SPARKLING WATER
- 20 G (2 TBSP, 0.71 OZ) SUNFLOWER OIL
- 1 LARGE EGG (1.76 OZ)
- 10 G (1 TBSP, 0.35 OZ) GRANULATED SUGAR
- ¼ TEASPOON OF SALT
- 100 G (⅔ CUP, 3.5 OZ) ICING SUGAR

1. Preheat the waffle maker on medium.
2. Place all the ingredients except the icing sugar in a large measuring cup, and blend with a hand blender to obtain a smooth batter.
3. Grease the waffle maker with some butter. Scoop a ladleful of batter into the centre (90 g (3.2 oz) of batter). Spread the batter with a plastic spoon. Close the waffle maker, and bake for 4 to 5 minutes until the waffle is crispy and golden brown. If you notice that your waffle is done after a few minutes, turn down the temperature a little.
4. Dust with a thin layer of icing sugar. Eat the waffles while they are still warm and crispy. That's when they are most delicious!

TIP

For a fun twist, serve with a dollop of Chantilly cream and fresh fruit.

SPECULOOS HEART-SHAPED WAFFLES

FOR 15 HEARTS

- 110 G (7 TBSP, 3.9 OZ) BUTTER
- 110 G (½ CUP, 3.9 OZ) DARK BROWN SUGAR
- 25 G (3 TBSP, 0.88 OZ) WATER
- 220 G (1 ½ CUP, 7.8 OZ) SELF-RISING FLOUR (SEE PASTRY BASICS, P. 29)
- 5 G (1 TSP, 0.18 OZ) CINNAMON

1. Preheat the waffle maker on medium.
2. In a bowl, beat the butter until soft. Add the other ingredients, and mix everything with your hands while squeezing to form an even dough. Do not knead.
3. Weigh out 15 portions of 30 g (1.06 oz) each, and shape into balls.
4. Brush the waffle maker well with softened butter. Place a ball of dough on each heart, and close the waffle maker. Press down until the waffle maker is completely closed. Bake for a few minutes until the waffle feels firm.
5. Open the waffle maker, and use a plastic knife to separate the hearts. Using a plastic palette knife, remove each individual heart from the waffle maker, and transfer them to a flat plate. Leave to cool, and store in an airtight container.

VEGAN HEART-SHAPED WAFFLES

FOR 15 HEARTS

- 110 G (7 TBSP, 3.9 OZ) MARGARINE
- 110 G (½ CUP, 3.9 OZ) GRANULATED SUGAR
- 25 G (3 TBSP, 0.88 OZ) WATER
- 220 G (1 ½ CUP, 7.8 OZ) SELF-RISING FLOUR (SEE PASTRY BASICS, P. 29)
- 5 G (1 TSP, 0.18 OZ) VANILLA SUGAR

1. Preheat the waffle maker on medium.
2. In a bowl, beat the margarine until soft. Add the other ingredients, and mix everything with your hands while squeezing to form an even dough. Do not knead.
3. Weigh out 15 portions of 30 g (1.06 oz) each, and shape into balls.
4. Brush the waffle maker well with softened butter. Place a ball of dough on each heart, and close the waffle maker, pressing down until it is completely closed. Bake for a few minutes until the waffle feels firm.
5. Open the waffle maker, and use a plastic knife to separate the hearts. Using a plastic palette knife, remove each individual heart from the waffle maker, and transfer them to a flat plate. Leave to cool, and store in an airtight container.

> **TIP**
>
> *For vegan speculoos waffles, substitute the granulated sugar with dark brown sugar and the vanilla with cinnamon.*

CHOCOLATE-DIPPED PARISIAN HEART-SHAPED WAFFLES

FOR 15 HEARTS

- 75 G (5 TBSP, 2.5 OZ) UNSALTED BUTTER, ROOM TEMPERATURE
- 1 ¼ SMALL EGG (2.1 OZ)
- 90 G (½ CUP, 3.2 OZ) GRANULATED SUGAR
- 5 G (1 TSP, 0.18 OZ) VANILLA SUGAR
- A PINCH OF SALT
- 145 G (1 CUP, 5.1 OZ) SELF-RISING FLOUR (SEE PASTRY BASICS, P. 29)
- 150 G (1 CUP, 5.3 OZ) MILK CHOCOLATE (CHOPPED)
- 50 G (⅓ CUP, 1.76 OZ) CHOCOLATE CURLS (SEE PASTRY BASICS, P. 25)

1. In a bowl, beat the butter until soft. Combine the egg with the granulated sugar, vanilla sugar and pinch of salt, and beat until you get a smooth batter. Add the flour, and continue beating until the batter is smooth.
2. Preheat the waffle maker on medium. Lightly brush with softened butter.
3. Fill a piping bag with a medium-sized non-serrated nozzle with the batter. Pipe mounds on each heart (25 grams (0.88 oz) per heart).
4. Bake for a few minutes until golden brown. Let the waffles cool.
5. Melt the milk chocolate *au bain-marie*, and dip half the waffles in the chocolate (10 g (0.35 oz) per waffle). Let the excess chocolate drip off, place the waffles on baking paper, and sprinkle with chocolate curls. They are ready for serving when the chocolate has solidified.

> **TIP**
>
> *You can make a nice hot chocolate milk with the leftover chocolate.*
>
> *The best way to remove the five waffles all at once from the waffle maker without breaking any is to first lift a waffle slightly with a knife and to then slowly slide a cake card under it.*

MINI VANILLA OR CHOCOLATE BUTTER WAFFLES

MAKES 20 TO 25 WAFFLES

- 120 G (8 TBSP, 4.2 OZ) UNSALTED BUTTER, ROOM TEMPERATURE
- 1 ½ LARGE (2.8 OZ) EGG
- 150 G (1 CUP, 5.3 OZ) SELF-RISING FLOUR (SEE PASTRY BASICS, P. 29)
- 100 G (½ CUP, 3.5 OZ) GRANULATED SUGAR
- 5 G (1 TBSP, 0.18 OZ) VANILLA SUGAR
- PINCH OF SALT
- 10 G (0.35 OZ) ICING SUGAR

Delicious, old-fashioned waffles with that full butter flavour. You'll find that people eat them faster than you can bake them.

1. Preheat a waffle maker with large diamond shapes on medium.
2. In a bowl, whisk the butter until fluffy. Add the other ingredients except the icing sugar, and mix until pipeable.
3. Lightly brush the waffle maker with softened butter. Fill a piping bag with a medium-sized non-serrated nozzle with the batter, and pipe mounds of about 20 g (0.71 oz) on each diamond shape. If the surface of the waffle maker is large enough, you can even pipe two mounds.
4. Bake for about 2 to 3 minutes until golden brown. Dust with icing sugar. The waffles are crispy but will become soft after cooling. Store in an airtight container.

TIP

For small chocolate butter waffles, mix 75 g (⅖ cup, 2.5 oz) pieces of chocolate for baking into the batter, and follow the same method. No need to dust them with icing sugar.

Place the dough in the freezer for half an hour. Use an ice-cream scoop to scoop balls of dough onto the waffle maker, and bake for about 2 to 3 minutes until golden brown.

CHOCOLATE-DIPPED LIÈGE WAFFLES

FOR 10 WAFFLES (75 G EACH)

- 25 G (0.88 OZ) FRESH YEAST OR 1 TBSP (0.32 OZ) INSTANT DRY YEAST
- 50 G (⅕ CUP, 1.76 OZ) WHOLE MILK
- 1 LARGE EGG (1.76 OZ)
- 300 G (2 CUPS, 10.6 OZ) ALL-PURPOSE FLOUR
- 25 G (2 ½ TBSP, 0.88 OZ) GRANULATED SUGAR
- 5 G (1 TSP, 0.18 OZ) VANILLA SUGAR
- 5 G (1 TSP, 0.18 OZ) SALT
- 150 G (10 TBSP, 5.3 OZ) UNSALTED BUTTER, ROOM TEMPERATURE
- 50 G (⅓ CUP, 1.76 OZ) BELGIAN PEARL SUGAR (P4) (SEE GLOSSARY, P. 32)
- 100 G (⅔ CUP, 3.5 OZ) CHOCOLATE BAKING DROPS
- 300 G (2 CUPS, 10.6 OZ) DARK OR MILK CHOCOLATE (CHOPPED)

Preparing Liège waffles can be a bit time-consuming. The dough needs to rise and can only be baked after an hour. But remember, patience is a virtue in baking!

1. Preheat a waffle maker with large, shallow diamond shapes on medium.
2. Crumble the yeast into a large bowl, add the milk and egg, and stir until dissolved. Mix in the flour, sugar, salt and butter to form a homogeneous mass.
3. Knead the dough on a work surface for 10 minutes until it feels smooth and no longer sticks to the work surface. Butter takes longer to absorb than water, which is why kneading dough with lots of butter usually takes a little longer. Let it rest for 10 minutes at room temperature.
4. Mix the pearl sugar and chocolate drops into the dough, and leave to rise for another 10 minutes.
5. Weigh out portions of dough (75 g (2.5 oz) each), shape them into balls, and let them rise for 45 to 60 minutes.
6. Bake the Liège waffles for about 3 minutes. No need to grease the waffle maker due to the large amount of butter in the dough. Let the waffles cool.
7. Melt the chocolate of your choice *au bain-marie*. Dip half the waffles in the chocolate (20 g of chocolate per waffle). Let the excess chocolate drip off, and place them on baking paper with the dipped chocolate side facing up. They are ready for serving when the chocolate has solidified.

TIP

You can make a nice hot chocolate milk with the leftover chocolate.

To clean the waffle maker quickly and thoroughly, mix 250 g (1 cup) of water with 250 g (1 ⅔ cup) of all-purpose flour into a batter that you pour onto the waffle maker while hot. Let it bake until done so that it absorbs any sugar residue on the waffle maker.

FLUFFY WAFFLES FOR STORING

FOR 8 WAFFLES
- 50 G (3 ½ TBSP, 1.76 OZ) UNSALTED BUTTER AT ROOM TEMPERATURE
- 1 ½ LARGE EGG (2.5 OZ)
- 90 G (½ CUP, 3.2 OZ) GRANULATED SUGAR
- 5 G (1 TSP, 0.18 OZ) VANILLA SUGAR
- 200 G (1 ⅓ CUP, 0.71 OZ) SELF-RISING FLOUR (SEE PASTRY BASICS, P. 29)

Everyone loves soft waffles, and they also make a great snack. A delicious easy recipe with ingredients everyone always has on hand. You can also easily store them in an airtight container for a while.

1. In a bowl, beat the butter until soft. Combine the egg with the granulated sugar and the vanilla sugar, and beat into a smooth batter. Add the flour, and mix with a spatula to form a dough.
2. Weigh out portions 50 g (1.76 oz) each, and shape into balls.
3. Preheat a waffle maker with large diamond shapes on medium. Lightly brush the waffle maker with softened butter.
4. Shape the balls into 8 cm (3.15 in) long sausage shapes, and place them on the waffle maker. Bake for 3 minutes until golden brown. The waffles are crispy but will become soft after cooling. Store in an airtight container.

IN THE BISCUIT TIN

Everyone can bake biscuits. Even people who don't think of themselves as bakers will enjoy it! Baking biscuits requires precision, which is how you are most likely to get a satisfactory result. Weigh the ingredients exactly as the recipe prescribes. The nice thing about baking biscuits is that you usually don't need to buy special ingredients. Resisting the urge to dip into the biscuit jar can be difficult. The biscuits all look so inviting, and the delicious smell alone makes your mouth water. Store all biscuits in a biscuit tin or airtight container so you can enjoy them for a long time.

LONG BUTTER SHORTBREAD BISCUITS (*BOTERTONGEN*)

MAKES 20 BISCUITS

- 100 G (7 TBSP, 3.5 OZ) UNSALTED BUTTER, ROOM TEMPERATURE
- 1.5 G SALT (¼ TSP)
- 50 G (3 ½ TBSP, 1.03 OZ) ICING SUGAR
- 160 G (1 CUP AND 1 TBSP, 5.6 OZ) ALL-PURPOSE FLOUR
- 1 EGG YOLK (0.71 OZ)
- 25 G (3 TBSP, 0.88 OZ) SHINY DECORATING SUGAR

These biscuits are very easy to make, and most people usually have all the ingredients on hand. So it's a great recipe if you want to whip up a sweet treat in no time at all. Even more so because they stay good for at last a month when stored in an airtight container or cookie jar. The secret to perfect, delicately crispy *botertongen*? Instead of kneading the dough, mix it quickly and briefly.

1. Line a baking tray with baking paper, and preheat the oven to 180°C (350°F).
2. Combine all the ingredients except the decorating sugar in a bowl, and mix with your fingers to form a homogeneous mass. Do not knead.
3. Roll the dough into a thick sausage shape 15 cm (5.90 in) long. Continue to roll the sausage shape in the decorating sugar until it is 20 cm (7.87 in) long. Press the roll to form a sheet of pastry measuring 8 × 20 cm (3.15 × 7.87 in), and refrigerate for half an hour to stiffen.
4. Cut the slice into 20 strips, and lay them on the baking tray.
5. Bake the biscuits for 12 to 14 minutes until golden brown.

TIP

For chocolate botertongen, *mix 75 g (½ cup, 2.7 oz) of chocolate baking drops into the dough.*

For cinnamon botertongen, *mix half a teaspoon of cinnamon into the dough.*

For lemon botertongen, *mix ¼ lemon zest into the dough.*

For vanilla botertongen, *mix 5 g (1 tsp) of vanilla sugar into the dough.*

You can make the dough in advance and store it in the freezer for several weeks. All you have to do when you want to bake some botertongen *is take a roll out of the freezer, defrost it for half hour at room temperature, cut it and bake it.*

COCONUT MACARONS

Do you have some leftover eggs? Instead of throwing them away, make these delicious chocolate/coconut macarons. A tasty riff on coconut Rochers.

FOR 20 MACARONS

- 150 G (¾ CUP, 5.3 OZ) GRANULATED SUGAR
- 2 ½ (3.5 OZ) LARGE EGG WHITES
- 100 G (⅔ CUP, 3.5 OZ) COCONUT POWDER
- 50 G (4 TBSP, 1.76 OZ) FINELY GROUND ALMOND MEAL
- 25 G (3 TBSP, 0.88 OZ) ICING SUGAR
- 200 G (1 CUP, 7.1 OZ) DARK CHOCOLATE (CHOPPED)

1. Line a baking tray with baking paper, and preheat the oven to 180°C (350°F).
2. In a pan over low heat, heat the sugar with the egg white until the sugar has dissolved. Add the coconut powder, and continue to heat the mixture to about 60°C. Remove the pan from the heat, and mix in the almond meal.
3. Fill a piping bag with a large non-serrated nozzle with the batter, and pipe mounds on the baking tray (20 g (0.71 oz) per serving). Sprinkle with icing sugar.
4. Place a Ø 5 cm (1.97 in) non-serrated round biscuit cutter over a mound of batter, and press to form a disc. Remove the cutter, and repeat with the rest of the batter.
5. Bake the macarons for 10 to 12 minutes until golden brown. Set aside to cool.
6. Melt the chocolate *au bain-marie*, and dip half the macaron in the chocolate. You can use the remaining chocolate for another recipe.

ALMOND HEARTS

FOR 20 HEARTS
- 2 ½ (3.5 OZ) LARGE EGG WHITES
- 60 G (5 TBSP, 2.1 OZ) GRANULATED SUGAR
- 240 G (8.5 OZ) *BROYAGE* (SEE PASTRY BASICS, P. 25)
- 60 G (⅔ CUP, 2.1 OZ) SLICED ALMONDS
- 200 G (7.1 OZ) BUTTERCREAM (SEE PASTRY BASICS, P. 25)
- 125 G (¾ CUP, 4.4 OZ) DARK CHOCOLATE (CHOPPED)
- 100 G (⅔ CUP, 3.5 OZ) CHOCOLATE CURLS (SEE PASTRY BASICS, P. 25)

These heart-shaped biscuits are made with two almond biscuits and a delicious cream in the middle. Half of the heart is coated with a nice crispy chocolate layer.

1. Line a baking tray with baking paper, and preheat the oven to 180°C (350°F).
2. Beat the egg whites, add the granulated sugar little by little, and beat until you have a firm meringue.
3. Using a spatula, fold the *broyage* into the meringue in two batches.
4. Fill a piping bag with a medium serrated nozzle with the batter and pipe 40 small hearts (10 g (3.5 oz) per heart). Sprinkle them with sliced almonds.
5. Bake the hearts for 10 to 12 minutes and let them cool.
6. Make the buttercream, and beat it until it is pipeable. Carefully turn over all the biscuits. Fill a piping bag with a small serrated nozzle. Pipe some buttercream on one biscuit, and place a second biscuit on top. Refrigerate the biscuits so the buttercream can set.
7. Melt the dark chocolate *au bain-marie*, dip half the biscuit in the chocolate, and sprinkle with chocolate curls.

TIP

This recipe is gluten-free.

MAKES 30 BISCUITS

- 110 G (7 TBSP, 3.9 OZ) UNSALTED BUTTER AT ROOM TEMPERATURE
- 3/4 (0.88 OZ) EGG WHITES
- 50 G (⅓ CUP, 1.76 OZ) ICING SUGAR
- A PINCH OF SALT
- 135 G (1 CUP, 4.8 OZ) ALL-PURPOSE FLOUR
- 15 BIGARREAU CHERRIES

CHERRY MARGUERITE

Cherry marguerites are old-fashioned shortbread biscuits. The cherry in the middle will brighten up your day! These biscuits are delicious, everyone loves them. Make them as a present and the recipient will love you forever.

1. Line a baking tray with baking paper, and preheat the oven to 180°C (350°F).
2. Beat the butter until fluffy. Add the egg whites, icing sugar, salt and flour. Mix the batter until pipeable. Use a spatula.
3. Transfer the batter to a piping bag with a large serrated nozzle. Pipe flowers onto a baking tray lined with baking paper (10 g (3.5 oz) of batter for each biscuit). When piping the flowers, make sure the piping bag points straight down. Decorate the centre of the flower with a half Bigarreau.
4. Bake the cherry biscuits for 12 to 14 minutes until golden brown.

FLEMISH *SPECULOOS*

FOR 40 BISCUITS
- 200 G (7.1 OZ) UNSALTED BUTTER, ROOM TEMPERATURE
- 300 G (2 CUPS, 10.6 OZ) ALL-PURPOSE FLOUR
- 5 G (1 TSP, 0.18 OZ) BAKING POWDER
- 200 G (1 CUP, 7.1 OZ) DARK BROWN SUGAR
- 5 G (1 TSP, 0.18 OZ) CINNAMON
- 40 G (3 TBSP, 1.41 OZ) GRANULATED SUGAR

Speculoos and coffee go together like peas and carrots. Depending on how you like it, you can cut the *speculoos* into thin slices for finer biscuits or thicker ones for sturdier *speculoos*.

1. Line a baking tray with baking paper, and preheat the oven to 180°C (350°F).
2. Beat the butter until fluffy. Combine the flour, baking powder and dark brown sugar, and add them to the butter. Mix well to form a homogeneous dough; do not knead it.
3. Roll the dough into a thick sausage shape 25 cm (9.85 in) long. Continue to roll the sausage shape in the granulated sugar until it is 40 cm (15.75 in) long. Press the roll to a width of 6 cm (2.36 in), and refrigerate for half an hour to stiffen.
4. Cut the dough into 40 slices each 1 cm (0.39 in) wide, turn them over, and place them on the baking tray.
5. Bake the biscuits for 12 to 14 minutes.

SPECULOOS BISCUITS (VEGAN)

FOR 40 BISCUITS
- 200 G (7.1 OZ) GOOD-QUALITY MARGARINE, ROOM TEMPERATURE
- 300 G (2 CUPS, 10.6 OZ) ALL-PURPOSE FLOUR
- 5 G (1 TSP, 0.18 OZ) BAKING POWDER
- 200 G (1 CUP, 7.1 OZ) DARK BROWN SUGAR
- 5 G (1 TSP, 0.18 OZ) CINNAMON
- 40 G (3 TBSP, 1.41 OZ) GRANULATED SUGAR

These vegan *speculoos* biscuits are easy to prepare. They taste just as good as the regular *speculoos,* and everyone can tuck into them.

1. Line a baking tray with baking paper and preheat the oven to 180°C (350°F).
2. Beat the margarine until fluffy. Combine the flour, baking powder and dark brown sugar, and add them to the margarine. Mix well to form a homogeneous dough; do not knead it.
3. Roll the dough into a thick sausage shape 25 cm (9.85 in) long. Continue to roll the sausage shape in the granulated sugar until it is 40 cm (15.75 in) long. Press the roll to a width of 6 cm (2.36 in), and refrigerate for half an hour to stiffen.
4. Cut the dough into 40 slices each 1 cm (0.39 in) wide, turn them over, and place them on the baking tray.
5. Bake the biscuits for 12 to 14 minutes.

SMALL SHORTBREAD COOKIES (VEGAN)

FOR 25 BISCUITS

- 120 G (¾ CUP, 4.2 OZ) ALL-PURPOSE FLOUR
- 80 G (5 TBSP, 2.8 OZ) GOOD-QUALITY MARGARINE
- 40 G (3 TBSP, 1.41 OZ) ICING SUGAR
- 1.5 G (⅓ TSP) SALT

Happiness is a biscuit away, or so they say. This recipe is a variation on English shortbread biscuits but completely vegan.

1. Line a baking tray with baking paper, and preheat the oven to 180°C (350°F).
2. In a bowl, mix all the ingredients together into a homogeneous mass while squeezing it with your fingers (squeeze hard!).
3. Roll the dough into a thick sausage shape 8 cm (3.15 in) long. Continue rolling the dough with a rolling pin until you have a 10 cm (3.93 in) square.
4. Divide the dough into 5 strips each measuring 2 × 10 cm (0.79 × 3.93 in). Divide each strip into 5 little squares each measuring 2 × 2 cm (0.79 × 0.39 in), and transfer the biscuits to the baking tray.
5. Bake the vegan biscuits for 12 to 14 minutes until golden brown.

SWEET AND CRISPY BISCUITS

MAKES 40 BISCUITS

- 135 G (4.8 OZ) UNSALTED BUTTER AT ROOM TEMPERATURE
- 75 G (3/5 CUP, 2.7 OZ) ICING SUGAR
- 10 G (2 TSP, 0.35 OZ) VANILLA SUGAR
- THE ZEST OF 1/4 LEMON
- 1 1/2 EGG YOLK (1.06 OZ)
- 180 G (1 1/5 CUP, 6.3 OZ) ALL-PURPOSE FLOUR
- 1 G (1/4 TSP) SALT
- 50 G (4 TBSP, 1.76 OZ) CANE SUGAR

This is a light, thin biscuit for when you're peckish or need a sweet break. You can eat this simple and delicate biscuit as is, but there are lots of variations possible. Add chopped chocolate or dip the biscuits in melted chocolate after baking. But first, try this basic recipe!

1. Line a baking tray with baking paper, and preheat the oven to 180°C (350°F).
2. Put all the ingredients except the cane sugar in a bowl, and mix while squeezing to form a dough mass. Do not knead.
3. Sprinkle the cane sugar on a towel, and roll the dough in the sugar to form a 40 cm (15.75 in) sausage shape. Refrigerate for an hour so the dough stiffens.
4. Cut the roll into 40 slices. Place on a baking tray.
5. Bake for 10 to 12 minutes until golden brown.

ACORNS

These acorns with chocolate have been doing the rounds for a long time. I got this recipe from my old *patron*.

MAKES 16 ACORNS
- 1 BIG EGG YOLK (0.88 OZ)
- 100 G (3.5 OZ) *BROYAGE* (SEE PASTRY BASICS, P. 25)
- 20 G (0.71 OZ) MELTED TEMPERED DARK CHOCOLATE (SEE GLOSSARY, P. 33)
- 20 G (0.71 OZ) CHOCOLATE FLAKES

1. Line one baking tray with baking paper, leaving the other unlined.
2. In a bowl, slowly mix the egg yolks into the *broyage* using your fingers. The dough will feel sticky, so let it dry out a little at room temperature for half an hour.
3. Divide the dough into 8 portions of 15 g (0.53 oz) each. Shape into balls, then form into 5 cm (1.97 in) long ovals. Cut them in half, transfer them to a plate with the flat side facing down, and refrigerate for about two hours.
4. Preheat the oven to 230°C (450°F).
5. Place the biscuits on a baking tray lined with baking paper. Slide a cold empty baking tray into the oven, and place the tray with the biscuits on top of it. That way, the bottom of the biscuits will not colour as quickly. Bake the acorns for about 8 to 10 minutes until golden brown.
6. When cooled, dip the flat part in melted chocolate and then in the chocolate flakes.

MAKES 20 BISCUITS

- 150 G (1 ¼ CUP, 5.3 OZ) GROUND ALMONDS
- 300 G (2 ¼, 10.6 OZ) ICING SUGAR
- 1 LARGE EGG WHITE (1.41 OZ)
- 10 G (2 TSP, 0.35 OZ) ORANGE ZEST

RICCIARELLI

These traditional soft and chewy biscuits come from Italy, more specifically from the province of Siena. They look like marzipan because they are made from almonds, sugar and egg whites. This pastry is said to date back as far as the fourteenth century, when an Italian knight named Ricciardetto Della Gherardesca ordered his cook to make these biscuits upon his return from the Crusades to his castle in Volterra. They reminded him of the shape of the shoes that people wore in the Middle East. This recipe is gluten-free.

1. Line a baking tray with baking paper, and preheat the oven to 180°C (350°F).
2. In a bowl, with your hands, mix the ground almonds with 200 g (7.1 oz) of icing sugar, the egg whites and the orange zest. The dough will feel sticky.
3. Sprinkle the rest of the icing sugar on a large plate. Using a teaspoon, scoop out portions of dough (20 g (0.71 oz) each) from the bowl and place them on top of the icing sugar. Roll each scoop in the icing sugar. Shape into balls and place on the baking tray. Press lightly.
4. Bake the *ricciarelli* for 15 to 18 minutes.

MARQUISETTES

FOR 30 BISCUITS

- 180 G (6.3 OZ) UNSALTED BUTTER, ROOM TEMPERATURE
- 90 G (¾ CUP, 3.2 OZ) ICING SUGAR
- 40 G (4 TBSP, 1.41 OZ) LUKEWARM WATER
- 270 G (1 ¾ CUP, 9.5 OZ) ALL-PURPOSE FLOUR
- A PINCH OF SALT
- 350 G (2 CUPS, 12.3 OZ) DARK CHOCOLATE (CHOPPED)

These biscuits are similar to the Dutch *sprits* biscuits. These serrated light biscuits originally come from Germany. The word *sprits* is a corruption of *Spritzkuchen*, which literally means 'piped pastry'. The chocolate finish makes these biscuits even more addictive.

1. Line a baking tray with baking paper, and preheat the oven to 180°C (350°F).
2. Beat the butter until fluffy with the icing sugar. Add the water, flour and a pinch of salt. Mix the batter until pipeable. Use a spatula.
3. Transfer the batter to a piping bag with a large serrated nozzle. Pipe 8 cm long strips onto the baking tray (20 g (0.71 oz) of batter to a biscuit).
4. Bake the biscuits for 12 to 14 minutes until golden brown. Let them cool down.
5. Melt the chocolate *au bain-marie*, and dip both ends in the melted dark chocolate.

BELGIAN TRUFFLES

MAKES 30 TRUFFLES

- 150 G (1 CUP, 5.3 OZ) DARK CHOCOLATE (CHOPPED)
- 150 G (⅗ CUP, 5.3 OZ) CREAM (40% FAT)
- 150 G (5.3 OZ) BUTTER, ROOM TEMPERATURE
- 250 G (1⅔ CUP) DARK CHOCOLATE (CHOPPED)
- 100 G (3.5 OZ) COCOA POWDER

The classic Belgian truffle is made of a creamy ganache coated in dark chocolate. The flavour is further enhanced by a fine dusting of cocoa powder. These truffles are a true delicacy, and people come from far and wide to taste them.

1. Boil the cream. Remove it from the heat and add the 150 g (1 cup, 5.3 oz) of chopped chocolate. Beat the butter until fluffy, and mix it into the chocolate mixture. Let the mixture cool to a smooth chocolate pasta.
2. Fill a piping bag with a Ø 1 cm (0.39 in) non-serrated nozzle, and pipe three 40 cm (15.75 in) long strips on a plate lined with baking paper. Let the dough harden in the freezer.
3. Melt the 250 g (1⅔ cup) dark chocolate *au bain-marie*, and temper it (see Glossary, p. 33). Spoon the cocoa onto a plate lined with baking paper.
4. Using a heated knife, cut each 40 cm strip into 10 shorter ones each measuring 4 cm (0.14 oz). Dip these strips in the chocolate, and roll them in the cocoa. Store the truffles in the refrigerator.

TIP

Use any leftover chocolate and cocoa powder for another recipe. Alternatively, you can also make some nice hot chocolate milk with it.

VANILLA *PAIN À LA GRECQUE*

FOR 15 BISCUITS

- 10 G (0.35 OZ) YEAST OR 1 TSP (0.13 OZ) INSTANT DRY YEAST
- 50 G (⅕ CUP) WHOLE MILK
- 25 G EGG (½ LARGE EGG, 0.88 OZ)
- 120 G (½ CUP, 4.2 OZ) ALL-PURPOSE FLOUR
- 50 G (3 TBSP, 1.76 OZ) UNSALTED BUTTER, ROOM TEMPERATURE
- 10 G (1 TBSP, 0.35 OZ) GRANULATED SUGAR
- 2.5 G (½ TSP, 0.09 OZ) SALT
- 5 G (1 TSP, 0.18 OZ) VANILLA SUGAR
- 50 G (4 TBSP, 1.76 OZ) SHINY DECORATING SUGAR
- 120 G (⅗ CUP, 4.2 OZ) CANE SUGAR

This is an old recipe which I inherited from my former *patron*, Jacques Bloch. The big difference with the Brussels *pain à la grecque* is that ours was made with decorating sugar, whereas the Brussels variant is coated with pearl sugar. To be honest, we think ours tastes better.

1. Line a baking tray with baking paper, and preheat the oven to 200°C (400°F).
2. Put the yeast in a bowl (if fresh yeast, crumble it), and stir in the milk and egg until dissolved. Add the rest of the ingredients except the shiny decorating sugar and the cane sugar, and mix everything into a homogeneous mass. Knead the dough on the work surface for 1 minute. The dough will feel sticky.
3. Divide the dough into 3 portions of 90 g (3.2 oz) each. Sprinkle the shiny decorating sugar on a clean towel, and roll the sausage-shaped dough through it until each sausage is 25 cm (9.85 in) long.
4. Remove the remaining decorating sugar from the towel, and sprinkle the cane sugar onto the towel in a 25 cm (9.85 in) long strip. Lay a strip of dough on the cane sugar, then press it into the sugar, and flatten it into a 10 × 25 cm (3.93 × 9.85 in) rectangle. Turn the dough over a few times. You can also roll it out with a rolling pin.
5. Place the sheet of dough on the baking paper, and cut it into five 5 × 10 cm (1.97 × 3.93 in) strips. Repeat with the other two sheets.
6. Bake for 12 to 14 minutes. Leave to cool on the baking paper. Store in an airtight container.

A CAKE
FIT FOR A KING

These recipes are so good that they would not look out of place during a tea party at the royal palace. They are also some of my favourite recipes. What's more, they are easy to make, everyone loves them, and you can play with the flavours. The secret to this dough is very simple: don't overmix it! Use the whisk to cream the butter. Then switch to a spatula. An overly fluffy batter will make the cake rise faster in the oven, but it will collapse when you take it out.

LEMON BUNDT CAKE WITH LEMON FROSTING

The best lemon cake ever. A sweet cake with a nice zingy lemon flavour and an amazing topping.

FOR 1 CAKE; SERVES 8

- SOFT BUTTER
- FLOUR
- 125 G (8 TBSP, 4.2 OZ) UNSALTED BUTTER, ROOM TEMPERATURE
- 100 G (⅔ CUP, 3.5 OZ) SELF-RISING FLOUR (SEE PASTRY BASICS, P. 29)
- 100 G (½ CUP, 3.5 OZ) GRANULATED SUGAR
- A PINCH OF SALT
- 2 LARGE EGGS (3.5 OZ)
- 10 G (2 TSP, 0.35 OZ) LEMON ZEST

TO GARNISH:
- 50 G (3 ½ TBSP, 1.76 OZ) BUTTER
- 90 G (½ CUP, 3.2 OZ) ICING SUGAR
- 10 G (1 TBSP, 0.35 OZ) LEMON JUICE
- 10 G (1 TBSP, 0.35 OZ) CREAM (40% FAT)

1. Grease a bundt cake tin (Ø 16 cm (6.29 in), 9 cm (3.54 in) high and 1.2 l capacity) generously with softened butter, dust with flour and preheat the oven to 180°C (350°F).
2. In a bowl, beat the unsalted butter until fluffy. Add the flour, sugar, lemon zest and pinch of salt, and stir with a spatula to make a smooth batter. Mix in the eggs in two batches, and stir vigorously with a spatula for a few minutes.
3. Fill a piping bag with a large non-serrated nozzle with the batter, and fill the baking tin.
4. Bake the cake for 35 to 40 minutes. After baking, immediately flip the cake upside down onto a plate, and leave to cool completely.
5. For the frosting, put the butter in a saucepan, and melt it over low heat. Add the icing sugar, lemon juice and cream, and continue to stir until the frosting reaches body temperature. Note: this doesn't take long.
6. Cover the cold cake with the frosting, and leave to set.

POPPY SEED AND WHITE CHOCOLATE GANACHE BUNDT CAKE

Blue poppy seed is obtained from the poppy plant. Poppy seeds and white chocolate are a perfect match.

FOR 1 CAKE; SERVES 8

- SOFT BUTTER
- FLOUR
- 125 G (8 TBSP, 4.2 OZ) UNSALTED BUTTER, ROOM TEMPERATURE
- 100 G (⅔ CUP, 3.5 OZ) SELF-RISING FLOUR (SEE PASTRY BASICS, P. 29)
- 100 G (½ CUP, 3.5 OZ) GRANULATED SUGAR
- A PINCH OF SALT
- 2 LARGE EGGS (3.5 OZ)
- 5 G (1 TSP, 0.18 OZ) LEMON ZEST
- 20 G (3 TBSP, 0.71 OZ) BLUE POPPY SEEDS (PLUS A LITTLE EXTRA FOR DECORATING)

TO GARNISH:
- 80 G (½ CUP, 2.8 OZ) WHITE CHOCOLATE (CHOPPED)
- 45 G (4 TBSP, 1.59 OZ) CREAM (40% FAT)

1. Grease a bundt-cake tin (Ø 16 cm (6.29 in), 9 cm (3.54 in) high and 1.2 l capacity) generously with softened butter, dust with flour, and preheat the oven to 180°C (350°F).
2. In a bowl, beat the unsalted butter until fluffy. Add the flour, sugar, lemon zest, poppy seeds and a pinch of salt, and stir with a spatula to make a smooth batter. Mix in the eggs in two batches, and stir vigorously with a spatula for a few minutes.
3. Fill a piping bag with a large non-serrated nozzle with the batter, and fill the baking tin.
4. Bake the cake for 35 to 40 minutes. After baking, immediately flip the cake upside down onto a plate, and leave to cool completely.
5. For the ganache, melt the white chocolate *au bain-marie* and mix in the cream. Pour over the cake and leave to set. Sprinkle some more poppy seeds on top of the ganache.

PECAN AND MILK CHOCOLATE GANACHE BUNDT CAKE

FOR 1 CAKE; SERVES 8

- SOFT BUTTER
- FLOUR
- 125 G (8 TBSP, 4.2 OZ) UNSALTED BUTTER, ROOM TEMPERATURE
- 100 G (2/3 CUP, 3.5 OZ) SELF-RISING FLOUR (SEE PASTRY BASICS, P. 29)
- 100 G (1/2 CUP, 3.5 OZ) GRANULATED SUGAR
- A PINCH OF SALT
- 2 LARGE EGGS (3.5 OZ)
- 200 G (1 2/3 CUP, 7.1 OZ) CHOPPED PECANS

TO GARNISH:
- 10 PECANS
- 80 G (1/2 CUP, 2.8 OZ) MILK CHOCOLATE (CHOPPED)
- 45 G (4 TBSP, 1.59 OZ) CREAM (40% FAT)

This pecan cake is as delicious as it sounds. Topped with a creamy layer of chocolate and some crunchy pecans!

1. Grease a bundt-cake tin (Ø 16 cm (6.29 in), 9 cm (3.54 in) high and 1.2 l capacity) generously with softened butter, dust with flour, and preheat the oven to 180°C (350°F).
2. In a bowl, beat the unsalted butter until fluffy. Add the flour, sugar and pinch of salt, and stir with a spatula to make a smooth batter. Mix in the eggs in two batches, and stir vigorously with a spatula for a few minutes. Stir in the chopped pecans.
3. Fill a piping bag with a large non-serrated nozzle with the batter, and fill the baking tin.
4. Bake the cake for 35 to 40 minutes. After baking, immediately flip the cake upside down onto a plate, and leave to cool completely.
5. For the ganache, melt the chocolate *au bain-marie,* and mix in the cream. Pour over the cake and leave to set. Garnish with pecans.

BANANA AND WALNUT BUNDT CAKE

FOR 1 CAKE; SERVES 8

- SOFT BUTTER
- FLOUR
- 100 G (7 TBSP, 3.05 OZ) UNSALTED BUTTER, ROOM TEMPERATURE
- 125 G (8 TBSP, 4.2 OZ) SELF-RISING FLOUR (SEE PASTRY BASICS, P. 29)
- 50 G (¼ CUP, 1.76 OZ) DARK BROWN SUGAR
- 25 G (2 ½ TBSP, 0.88 OZ) GRANULATED SUGAR
- A PINCH OF SALT
- 1 LARGE EGG (1.76 OZ)
- 100 G (3.5 OZ) RIPE BANANA, MASHED
- 60 G (½ CUP, 2.1 OZ) CHOPPED WALNUTS

If you have any old brown bananas sitting in your fruit bowl, try this perfect recipe for a delicious banana cake! Garnish with walnuts before serving this work of art.

1. Grease a bundt-cake tin (Ø 16 cm (6.29 in), 9 cm (3.54 in) high and 1.2 l capacity) generously with softened butter, dust with flour and preheat the oven to 180°C (350°F).
2. In a bowl, whisk the butter until fluffy. Add the flour, dark brown sugar, granulated sugar, banana puree and pinch of salt and stir with a spatula to make a smooth batter. Add the egg and stir vigorously with a spatula for a few minutes. Stir in 40 g (1.55 oz) of walnuts.
3. Sprinkle 20 g (0.71 oz) of walnuts on the bottom of the cake tin. Fill a piping bag with a large non-serrated nozzle with the batter and fill the baking tin.
4. Bake the cake for 50 to 55 minutes. After baking, immediately flip the cake upside down onto a plate and leave to cool completely.

> **TIP**
>
> *Make your banana bundt cake the day before. The nuts in the pastry will soften and you will find it easier to cut into the cake!*
>
> *The riper the banana, the better the flavour (bananas with brown spots are often preferred because they are sweeter).*

RASPBERRY AND CRUMBLE BUNDT CAKE

This raspberry bundt cake is always a hit. The summery flavours with the added crumble make it simply irresistible.

FOR 1 CAKE; SERVES 8

- SOFT BUTTER
- FLOUR
- 40 G (1.41 OZ) BUTTER CRUMBLE (SEE PASTRY BASICS, P. 25)
- 125 G (8 TBSP, 4.2 OZ) UNSALTED BUTTER, ROOM TEMPERATURE
- 100 G (⅔ CUP, 3.5 OZ) SELF-RISING FLOUR (SEE PASTRY BASICS, P. 29)
- 100 G (½ CUP, 3.5 OZ) GRANULATED SUGAR
- A PINCH OF SALT
- 2 LARGE EGGS (3.5 OZ)
- 5 G (1 TSP, 0.18 OZ) VANILLA SUGAR
- 100 G (3.5 OZ) FRESH RASPBERRIES

1. Grease a bundt-cake tin (Ø 16 cm (6.29 in), 9 cm (3.54 in) high and 1.2 l capacity) generously with softened butter, dust with flour, and preheat the oven to 180°C (350°F).
2. Make the crumble first.
3. In a bowl, beat the unsalted butter until fluffy. Add the flour, sugar, vanilla sugar and pinch of salt, and stir with a spatula to make a smooth batter. Mix in the eggs in two batches, and stir vigorously with a spatula for a few minutes.
4. Fill a piping bag with a large non-serrated nozzle with the batter. Spread the crumble on the bottom of the baking tin, and fill with half the batter. Push the raspberries into the centre of the batter. Add the remaining batter.
5. Bake the cake for 35 to 40 minutes. After baking, immediately flip the cake upside down onto a plate, and leave to cool completely.

TIP

Instead of raspberries, you can add strawberries, or red and blue forest fruit.

MILK CHOCOLATE AND *SPECULOOS* CRUMBLE MARBLE BUNDT CAKE

Marble cake is a fun combination of two popular cakes, namely plain cake and chocolate cake. The best of both worlds in one cake! The chocolate and speculoos garnish makes this cake even more unique.

FOR 1 CAKE; SERVES 8
- SOFT BUTTER
- FLOUR

FOR THE PLAIN CAKE BATTER:
- 75 G (5 TBSP, 2.5 OZ) UNSALTED BUTTER, ROOM TEMPERATURE
- 60 G (4 TBSP, 2.1 OZ) SELF-RISING FLOUR (SEE PASTRY BASICS, P. 29)
- 60 G (5 TBSP, 2.1 OZ) GRANULATED SUGAR
- 5 G (1 TSP, 0.18 OZ) VANILLA SUGAR
- A PINCH OF SALT
- 1 LARGE EGG (2.1 OZ)

FOR THE CHOCOLATE CAKE BATTER:
- 50 G (3 ½ TBSP, 1.7 OZ) UNSALTED BUTTER, ROOM TEMPERATURE
- 40 G (3 TBSP, 1.41 OZ) SELF-RISING FLOUR (SEE PASTRY BASICS, P. 29)
- 40 G (3 ½ TBSP, 1.41 OZ) GRANULATED SUGAR
- 10 G (1 TBSP, 0.36 OZ) WHOLE MILK
- 5 G (1 TSP, 0.18 OZ) COCOA POWDER
- A PINCH OF SALT
- 1 SMALL EGG (1.41 OZ)

TO GARNISH:
- SOME *SPECULOOS* (SEE FLEMISH *SPECULOOS*, P. 207)
- 80 G (½ CUP, 2.8 OZ) MILK CHOCOLATE (CHOPPED)
- 45 G (4 TBSP, 1.59 OZ) CREAM (40% FAT)

1. Grease a bundt-cake tin (Ø 16 cm (6.29 in), 9 cm (3.54 in) high and 1.2 l capacity) generously with softened butter, dust with flour, and preheat the oven to 180°C (350°F).
2. For the plain cake batter, beat the 75 g (2.5 oz) of unsalted butter in a bowl until fluffy. Add the flour, sugar, vanilla sugar and pinch of salt, and stir with a spatula to make a smooth batter. Mix in the egg, and stir vigorously with a spatula for a few minutes.
3. For the chocolate cake batter, beat the 50 g (1.7 oz) of unsalted butter in a bowl until fluffy. Add the flour, sugar, milk, cocoa powder and a pinch of salt, and stir with a spatula to make a smooth batter. Mix in the egg, and stir vigorously with a spatula for a few minutes.
4. Fill a piping bag with a large non-serrated nozzle with the batter as follows. A third plain cake batter, a third chocolate batter and repeat. Pipe the batter into the cake tin.
5. Bake the cake for 35 to 45 minutes. After baking, immediately flip the cake upside down onto a plate and leave to cool completely.
6. Crumble the *speculoos* biscuits. For the ganache, melt the chocolate *au bain-marie* and mix in the cream. Pour over the cake. Sprinkle the crumbled *speculoos* on top of the ganache, and leave to set.

> **TIP**
>
> *For a* speculoos *marble cake, substitute the cocoa in the chocolate batter with half a teaspoon of cinnamon. No need to add milk. You can also finish the cake with chocolate curls.*

A CAKE FIT FOR A KING

CHOCOLATE BUNDT CAKE

FOR 1 CAKE; SERVES 8

- SOFT BUTTER
- FLOUR
- 125 G (8 TBSP, 4.2 OZ) UNSALTED BUTTER, ROOM TEMPERATURE
- 100 G (⅔ CUP, 3.5 OZ) SELF-RISING FLOUR (SEE PASTRY BASICS, P. 29)
- 100 G (½ CUP, 3.5 OZ) GRANULATED SUGAR
- A PINCH OF SALT
- 2 LARGE EGGS (3.5 OZ)
- 20 G (2 TBSP, 0.71OZ) WHOLE MILK
- 10 G (2 TSP, 0.35 OZ) COCOA POWDER
- 100 G (⅔ CUP, 3.5 OZ) CHOCOLATE DROPS FOR BAKING

TO GARNISH:
- 60 G (⅓ CUP, 2.1 OZ) DARK CHOCOLATE (CHOPPED)
- 40 G (4 TBSP, 1.59 OZ) CREAM (40% FAT)

Does chocolate make you go bananas? Does the mere thought of chocolate drops, cocoa and dark chocolate combined in one recipe make your mouth water? Look no further; this is your new favourite cake!

1. Grease a bundt-cake tin (Ø 16 cm (6.29 in), 9 cm (3.54 in) high and 1.2 l capacity) generously with softened butter, dust with flour, and preheat the oven to 180°C (350°F).
2. In a bowl, whisk the butter until fluffy. Add the flour, whole milk, cocoa powder, sugar and a pinch of salt, and stir with a spatula to make a smooth batter. Mix in the eggs in two batches, and stir vigorously with a spatula for a few minutes. Stir in the chocolate drops.
3. Fill a piping bag with a large non-serrated nozzle with the batter, and fill the baking tin.
4. Bake the cake for 35 to 40 minutes. After baking, immediately flip the cake upside down onto a plate, and leave to cool completely.
5. For the ganache, melt the chocolate *au bain-marie* and mix in the cream. Pour over the cake and leave to set.

ALMOND BUNDT CAKE

FOR 1 CAKE; SERVES 8
- SOFT BUTTER
- 25 G SLICED ALMONDS
- 100 G (7 TBSP, 3.5 OZ) UNSALTED BUTTER, ROOM TEMPERATURE
- 75 G (½ CUP, 2.5 OZ) SELF-RISING FLOUR (SEE PASTRY BASICS, P. 29)
- 90 G (½ CUP, 3.2 OZ) GRANULATED SUGAR
- 40 G (3 TBSP, 1.41 OZ) ALMOND MEAL
- A PINCH OF SALT
- 1 LARGE AND 1 SMALL EGG (3.2 OZ)
- 5 G (1 TBSP, 0.18 OZ) ICING SUGAR

A cake with a twist! The heavenly, full almond flavour finished with toasted almonds and icing sugar adds a unique touch to this cake.

1. Generously grease a bundt-cake tin (Ø 16 cm (6.29 in), 9 cm (3.54 in) high and 1.2 l capacity) with softened butter, and sprinkle the sliced almonds into it. Preheat the oven to 180°C (350°F).
2. In a bowl, beat the unsalted butter until fluffy. Add the flour, sugar, almond meal and pinch of salt, and stir with a spatula to make a smooth batter. Mix in the eggs in two batches, and stir vigorously with a spatula for a few minutes.
3. Fill a piping bag with a large non-serrated nozzle with the batter, and fill the baking tin.
4. Bake the cake for 35 to 40 minutes. After baking, immediately flip the cake upside down onto a plate, and leave to cool completely. Dust with icing sugar.

REGAL CAKES

Cakes are a delicious treat for any occasion. Whether you opt for a classic apple and streusel cake, the tartness of blackberries and orange, or the exotic flavour of dried figs, there is always something to delight your guests' taste buds. Depending on the season, you can choose fresh seasonal produce or frozen fruit. That way, you can enjoy these delectable recipes any time of the year. You can also freeze these cakes so you can easily pull one out if you have unexpected visitors or are planning a party. Add the finishing touch – the apricot glaze – just before serving. These cakes can also sit out for several days without the quality being affected. The combination of delicious fruit, amazing fillings and rich decoration makes for a real taste sensation.

PEAR AND *BRÉSILIENNE* CAKE ROYALE

This recipe is made with tinned Conference pears in syrup. The pears are sweet and firm, so easy to cut. This is a juicy pear with a grainy texture. You can also use fresh pears, but make sure they are sufficiently ripe.

SERVES 8
- 5 PEAR HALVES IN SYRUP
- 75 G (5 TBSP, 2.7 OZ) APRICOT JAM FOR DECORATING (SEE PASTRY BASICS, P. 24)
- 10 G (1 TBSP, 0.35 OZ) *BRÉSILIENNE* NUTS (SEE PASTRY BASICS, P. 25)
- CAKE BASE AND FILLING (SEE PASTRY BASICS, P. 28)

1. Preheat the oven to 180°C (350°F).
2. Prepare the base and filling.
3. Cut the pears into strips, and arrange them in a fan shape on top of the filling.
4. Bake the royale for 40 minutes.
5. After baking, immediately brush with the apricot glaze. Sprinkle with *brésilienne* nuts, and leave the cake to cool.

APPLE AND STREUSEL CAKE ROYALE

SERVES 8

- 200 G (1 ¼ CUP, 7.1 OZ) CHOPPED APPLE (BOSKOOP, BRAMLEY, GRANNY SMITH)
- 150 G (¾ CUP, 5.3 OZ) STREUSEL (SEE PASTRY BASICS, P. 28)
- CAKE BASE AND FILLING (SEE PASTRY BASICS, P. 28)

I prefer to use cooking apples for this cake. That way, you will get an interesting sweet-and-sour combination. Boskoop apples (similar to Bramley) are a good choice. These are usually picked in September. You can also use a sweet apple such as a Jonagold, but the chopped apple will be quite soft after baking.

1. Preheat the oven to 180°C (350°F).
2. Prepare the base and filling.
3. Spread the chopped apple on top of the filling, and add a generous sprinkling of streusel on top.
4. Bake the royale for 40 minutes.

> **TIP**
>
> *You can dust the pastry with some icing sugar.*

APRICOT CAKE ROYALE

The tastiest apricots generally come from France.
For this recipe, I choose to go with tinned apricots in syrup, which are pitted and easy to use.

SERVES 8

- 350 G (1.23 OZ) APRICOT HALVES IN SYRUP
- 75 G (5 TBSP, 2.7 OZ) APRICOT JAM FOR DECORATING (SEE PASTRY BASICS, P. 24)
- CAKE BASE AND FILLING (SEE PASTRY BASICS, P. 28)

1. Preheat the oven to 180°C (350°F).
2. Prepare the base and filling.
3. Tip the apricots into a colander, and let them drain. Arrange them on top of the filling.
4. Bake the royale for 40 minutes.
5. After baking, immediately brush with the apricot glaze, and leave to cool.

BLACKBERRY CAKE ROYALE

Blackberries have a beautiful purple colour and are a good source of dietary fibre. Beware of parasites if you pick them in the wild, however. A safer option is to buy them in shops or from a professional grower.

SERVES 8

- 20 G (2 TBSP, 0.71 OZ) ORANGE ZEST
- 300 G (1 ¼ CUPS, 10.6 OZ) FROZEN BLACKBERRIES (FRESH IS ALSO AN OPTION)
- 75 G (5 TBSP, 2.7 OZ) APRICOT JAM FOR DECORATING (SEE PASTRY BASICS, P. 24)
- 10 G (2 TBSP, 0.35 OZ) ROASTED SLICED ALMONDS (SEE PASTRY BASICS, P. 26)
- SOME FRESH BLACKBERRIES FOR DECORATING YOUR CAKE
- CAKE BASE AND FILLING (SEE PASTRY BASICS, P. 28)

1. Preheat the oven to 180°C (350°F).
2. Prepare the base and filling. Mix the orange zest with the filling, and fill the base with it.
3. Tip the frozen fruit into a colander, let it thaw, and drain the liquid. Spread the fruit on top of the filling.
4. Bake the royale for 40 minutes.
5. After baking, immediately brush with the apricot glaze. Decorate with some almonds and fresh blackberries, and leave to cool.

FIG AND CRUMBLE CAKE ROYALE

SERVES 8

- 200 G (1 ¼ CUP, 7.1 OZ) DRIED FIGS, CUT INTO PIECES
- 80 G (½ CUP, 2.8 OZ) BUTTER CRUMBLE (SEE PASTRY BASICS, P. 25)
- EXTRA DRIED FIGS, CUT INTO PIECES TO DECORATE
- CAKE BASE AND FILLING (SEE PASTRY BASICS, P. 28)

I use dried figs for this recipe. Figs are sweet tasting and are grown in southern Europe. The vitamins, minerals and fibre promote good digestion.

1. Preheat the oven to 180°C (350°F).
2. Prepare the base and filling. Mix the chopped figs with the filling, and fill the base with it.
3. Sprinkle with the crumble.
4. Bake the royale for about 30 minutes at 180°C (350°F), and let cool. Decorate with some chopped figs.

RASPBERRY CAKE ROYALE

SERVES 8

- HALF A TEASPOON OF CINNAMON
- 300 G (2 CUPS, 10.6 OZ) FROZEN RASPBERRIES (FRESH IS ALSO AN OPTION)
- 75 G (5 TBSP, 2.7 OZ) APRICOT JAM FOR DECORATING (SEE PASTRY BASICS, P. 24)
- 10 G (2 TBSP, 0.35 OZ) ROASTED SLICED ALMONDS (SEE PASTRY BASICS, P. 26)
- SOME FRESH RASPBERRIES TO DECORATE YOUR CAKE
- CAKE BASE AND FILLING (SEE PASTRY BASICS, P. 28)

Did you know that you can also buy orange and yellow raspberries? They even sell summer raspberries and autumn raspberries. Raspberries need a lot of sunlight to ripen. After picking the fruit, store it in a dry place.

1. Preheat the oven to 180°C (350°F).
2. Prepare the base and filling. Mix the cinnamon with the filling, and fill the base with it.
3. Tip the frozen fruit into a colander, let it thaw, and drain the liquid. Spread the fruit on top of the filling.
4. Bake the royale for 40 minutes.
5. After baking, immediately brush with the apricot glaze. Decorate with some almonds and fresh raspberries, and leave to cool.

REDCURRANT CAKE ROYALE

SERVES 8

- 300 G (2 CUPS, 10.6 OZ) FROZEN REDCURRANT BERRIES (FRESH IS ALSO AN OPTION)
- 75 G (5 TBSP, 2.7 OZ) APRICOT JAM FOR DECORATING (SEE PASTRY BASICS, P. 24)
- 10 G (2 TBSP, 0.35 OZ) ROASTED SLICED ALMONDS (SEE PASTRY BASICS, P. 26)
- SOME FRESH BERRIES FOR DECORATING
- CAKE BASE AND FILLING (SEE PASTRY BASICS, P. 28)

Redcurrants are picked from late June to August. Don't pick them too early! That way, they are not too sour. These berries are a good source of vitamins and are easy to grow. You can tell they are ripe when they are completely red.

1. Preheat the oven to 180°C (350°F).
2. Prepare the base and filling.
3. Tip the frozen fruit into a colander, let it thaw, and drain the liquid. Spread the fruit on top of the filling.
4. Bake the royale for 40 minutes.
5. After baking, immediately brush with the apricot glaze. Decorate with some almonds and redcurrants, and leave to cool.

FOREST FRUIT CAKE ROYALE

SERVES 8

- 350 G (2 ½ CUPS, 12.3 OZ) MIXED FOREST FRUITS FROM THE FREEZER (FRESH IS ALSO AN OPTION)
- 75 G (5 TBSP, 2.7 OZ) APRICOT JAM FOR DECORATING (SEE PASTRY BASICS, P. 24)
- 10 G (2 TBSP, 0.35 OZ) ROASTED SLICED ALMONDS (SEE PASTRY BASICS, P. 26)
- SOME FRESH FRUIT TO DECORATE THE CAKE
- CAKE BASE AND FILLING (SEE PASTRY BASICS, P. 28)

If you can't choose between the glut of summer fruit that you can get nowadays, then this is the cake for you! The combination of redcurrants, strawberries, blackberries, raspberries, blackcurrants and blueberries adds a rich, varied flavour. You can easily find this mix in the freezer section of most supermarkets. Remember to let the fruit thaw through and drain before using it so that the cake is baked through and does not get soggy.

1. Preheat the oven to 180°C (350°F).
2. Prepare the base and filling.
3. Tip the frozen fruit into a colander, let it thaw, and drain the liquid. Spread the fruit on top of the filling.
4. Bake the royale for 40 minutes.
5. After baking, immediately brush with the apricot glaze. Decorate with some almonds and summer fruit, and leave to cool.

DELICIOUS SAVOURY BAKES

Last but not least, it's time for some savoury treats! The array of savoury options which you can add to your brunch or aperitif table is endless. Obviously, there are too many to choose from, but in this chapter I have shared some recipes for some mouth-watering choices, with lots of variations. Get started with these. Obviously, nothing stops you from experimenting with flavours. That way, you can put together a dazzling array for a party buffet with a wow factor.

SAVOURY FLATBREAD

These savoury flatbreads look a bit like tiny pizzas, with their round dough base on which you can spoon any type of topping. This recipe dates back to the time when women would bake their daily bread in the communal oven in the morning and then use it for different kinds of meals throughout the day.

BASIC RECIPE FOR 10 FLATBREADS (100 G (3.5 OZ) EACH) (VEGAN)

- 375 G (1 ½ CUP, 13.3 OZ) WATER
- 25 G (0.88 OZ) FRESH YEAST OR 1 TBSP (0.32 OZ) INSTANT DRY YEAST
- 625 G (4 CUPS, 22 OZ) BREAD FLOUR
- 15 G (1 ½ TBSP, 0.53 OZ) OLIVE OIL
- 10 G (2 TSP, 0.35 OZ) SALT
- SOME FLOUR FOR DUSTING
- 20 G (2 ½, 0.71 OZ) OLIVE OIL FOR BRUSHING
- 10 G (1 TBSP, 0.35 OZ) COARSE SEA SALT

1. Preheat the oven to 225°C (435°F).
2. Put the yeast into a large bowl (if fresh yeast, crumble it), add water, and stir until completely dissolved. Mix in the bread flour, salt and 15 g olive oil to obtain a homogeneous mixture.
3. Pour out the dough on the work surface, and knead for 6 minutes until elastic. Let it rest for 10 minutes at room temperature.
4. Divide the dough into 10 portions of 100 g (3.5 oz) each, shape into balls, and leave to rise for 20 minutes.
5. Dust your work surface with some flour. Using a rolling pin, roll the dough balls into Ø 16 cm (6.29 in) discs. Brush the baking tray with the olive oil, and sprinkle with some sea salt. Arrange the bases on the baking tray, and decorate with a topping of your choice. Let rise for an hour.
6. Bake for 8 to 10 minutes.

TIP

Do not bake the flatbread for too long, as the edges will harden.

MOZZARELLA AND HALVED CHERRY TOMATOES

- 200 G (¾ CUP, 6.5 OZ) OLIVE OIL
- A MIXTURE OF 2 G (2 TSP) DRIED OREGANO AND 2 G (2 TSP) DRIED BASIL
- 400 G (14.1 OZ) GRATED MOZZARELLA
- 500 G (3 CUPS, 17.6 OZ) HALVED CHERRY TOMATOES
- 2 G DRIED OREGANO EXTRA

1. Brush the flatbread with olive oil, and sprinkle with the herbs.
2. Garnish with the sliced mozzarella and tomatoes.
3. Season the oven cake with a little extra oregano after baking.

GREEK-STYLE

- 200 G (¾ CUP, 6.5 OZ) OLIVE OIL
- 4 G (2 TSP) DRIED OREGANO
- 200 G (7.1 OZ) GRATED EMMENTAL CHEESE
- 200 G (1 CUP, 7.1 OZ) PITTED BLACK OLIVES, SLICED
- 200 G (7.1 OZ) GRATED MOZZARELLA
- 50 G (5 TBSP, 1.7 OZ) CAPERS
- GROUND BLACK PEPPER

1. Brush the flatbread with olive oil, and sprinkle with the oregano.
2. Garnish with Emmental cheese, olives, mozzarella and capers.
3. Season with some ground black pepper.

MEDITERRANEAN-STYLE

- 200 G (¾ CUP, 6.5 OZ) OLIVE OIL
- 1 CLOVE OF GARLIC
- A MIXTURE OF 2 G (2 TSP) DRIED OREGANO AND 2 G (2 TSP) DRIED BASIL
- 500 G (3 CUPS, 17.6 OZ) CHERRY TOMATOES
- 200 G (7.1 OZ) ANCHOVIES, CUT INTO PIECES

1. Mix the olive oil with the minced garlic.
2. Brush the flatbread with the mixture, and sprinkle with the herbs.
3. Garnish with the cherry tomatoes and the anchovies.

EMMENTAL AND BACON STRIPS

- 200 G (¾ CUP, 6.5 OZ) OLIVE OIL
- A MIXTURE OF 2 G (2 TSP) DRIED OREGANO AND 2 G (2 TSP) DRIED BASIL
- 400 G (14.1 OZ) GRATED EMMENTAL CHEESE
- 400 G (14.1 OZ) LIGHTLY SMOKED BACON STRIPS

1. Brush the flatbread with olive oil, and sprinkle with the herbs.
2. Sprinkle with the Emmental, and garnish with the bacon strips.

SALMON AND CHIVES

- 500 G (2 CUPS, 17.6 OZ) QUARK CHEESE
- 100 G (⅖ CUP, 3.5 OZ) CREAM (40% FAT)
- 1 G (⅓ TSP) NUTMEG, 1 G (⅓ TSP) GROUND BLACK PEPPER AND 5 G (1 TSP) SALT
- 300 G (10.6 OZ) SMOKED SALMON
- 20 G (3 TBSP, 0.71 OZ) MINCED CHIVES

1. Combine the quark with the cream and herbs.
2. Spread the cheese mixture on the flatbread.
3. Garnish with the smoked salmon and the chives.

ROSEMARY AND COARSE SEA SALT (VEGAN)

- 200 G (¾ CUP, 6.5 OZ) OLIVE OIL
- 1 CLOVE OF GARLIC
- 3 G (2 TBSP, 0.11 OZ) FINELY CHOPPED FRESH ROSEMARY
- 5 G (1 TSP, 0.18 OZ) COARSE SEA SALT

1. Mix the olive oil with the chopped garlic, and brush the oven flatbread with it.
2. Sprinkle with the rosemary and coarse salt.

PECORINO CHEESE

- 200 G (¾ CUP, 6.5 OZ) OLIVE OIL
- A MIXTURE OF 2 G (2 TSP) DRIED OREGANO AND 2 G (2 TSP) DRIED BASIL
- 400 G (14.1 OZ) GRATED PECORINO CHEESE

1. Brush the flatbread with olive oil, and sprinkle with the herbs and sea salt.
2. Sprinkle with the pecorino.

RED ONION

- 500 G (2 CUPS, 17.6 OZ) QUARK CHEESE
- 100 G (⅖ CUP, 3.5 OZ) CREAM (40% FAT)
- 1 G (⅓ TSP) NUTMEG, 1 G (⅓ TSP) GROUND BLACK PEPPER AND 5 G (1 TSP) SALT
- 200 G (7.1 OZ) RED ONION, SLICED

1. Combine the quark with the cream and herbs.
2. Spread the cheese mixture on the flatbread.
3. Garnish with the red onion.

TIP

Sprinkle some bacon on top of the filling.

PIZZA TARTELETTE

You'll love these mini tarts once you've made them! Line mini tart tins with the dough and fill them with the most delicious ingredients. If you make the pizzas in advance, reheat them briefly in the oven (never in the microwave!) for best results. The outside of the pizzas will become nice and crispy after baking, while the filling remains deliciously soft.

BASIC RECIPE FOR 5 TARTS
- 200 G (7.1 OZ) SALTED BRIOCHE DOUGH (SEE PASTRY BASICS, P. 26)
- 150 G (5.3 OZ) PIZZA SAUCE (SEE PASTRY BASICS, P. 27)

1. Grease 5 round mini tart tins (Ø 10 cm (3.93 in) and 2.5 cm (1 in) high) with butter and preheat the oven to 220°C (425°F).
2. Make the brioche dough, divide it into 5 portions of 40 g (1.41 oz) each, and shape into balls. Roll out the balls with the rolling pin into Ø 12 cm (4.72 in) discs.
3. Line the baking tins with the dough, and push the edges up a little with your thumbs. Fill each of the tart tins with 30 g (2 tbsp, 1.06 oz) of pizza sauce, and add your toppings.
4. Bake for 12 to 15 minutes at 220°C (425°F).

> **TIP**
>
> *You can eat the pizzas immediately. However, you'll find that the crust is quite soft, which is why I recommend baking them in advance. Afterwards, reheat the cold pizza in a preheated oven at 180°C (350°F) for 15 minutes. The crust will become nice and crispy, enhancing the flavour.*

TOMATO, MOZZARELLA AND OLIVE TART

- 1 LARGE TOMATO, SLICED
- A PINCH OF GROUND BLACK PEPPER
- A PINCH OF SALT
- 5 TSP OLIVE OIL
- 150 G (5.3 OZ) MOZZARELLA
- 75 G (⅓ CUP, 2.5 OZ) PITTED BLACK OLIVES, SLICED
- 5 G (2 TSP, 0.18 OZ) DRIED OREGANO

1. Arrange the tomato slices on top of the pizza sauce. Season with salt and pepper, and drizzle with olive oil.
2. Thinly slice the mozzarella, and arrange it on top of the tomato slices.
3. Sprinkle the sliced black olives over the cheese, garnish with cherry tomatoes, and season with oregano.
4. Bake for 12 to 15 minutes at 220°C (425°F).

COURGETTE-AND-GOAT-CHEESE TART

- 50 G (5 TBSP, 1.76 OZ) OLIVE OIL
- 1 COURGETTE, DICED
- A PINCH OF GROUND BLACK PEPPER
- A PINCH OF SALT
- 100 G (3.5 OZ) GOAT'S CHEESE, DICED
- 2 CLOVES OF GARLIC

1. Put a generous amount of olive oil in a pan and fry the diced courgette with the minced garlic until tender. Season with salt and pepper.
2. Spread the diced courgette on top of the sauce, and sprinkle with the goat cheese.
3. Bake for 12 to 15 minutes at 220°C (425°F).

PROVENÇAL TART

- 200 G (7.1 OZ) MINCE (½ BEEF AND ½ VEAL)
- 5 TSP OLIVE OIL
- A PINCH OF GROUND BLACK PEPPER
- A PINCH OF SALT
- ¼ RED AND ¼ GREEN PEPPER
- 5 MUSHROOMS, SLICED
- 1 TSP DRIED OREGANO
- 1 TSP DRIED BASIL
- 50 G (1.76 OZ) GRATED EMMENTAL CHEESE
- A PINCH OF SATAY SPICES
- A PINCH OF PROVENÇAL HERBS

1. Fry the mince in olive oil with some salt and pepper and leave to cool.
2. Spread the mince over the pizza sauce, and add some diced green and red peppers and sliced mushrooms. Season with a mixture of oregano and basil. Sprinkle with grated cheese.
3. Bake for 12 to 15 minutes at 220°C (425°F). After baking, season to taste with some satay spices and Provençal herbs.

CHICKEN TART

- 200 G COOKED CHICKEN, CUT INTO PIECES
- 100 G (3.5 OZ) PIZZA SAUCE
- ¼ RED AND ¼ GREEN PEPPER
- 40 G (1.41 OZ) GRATED EMMENTAL CHEESE
- 5 MUSHROOMS
- A PINCH OF PEPPER
- A PINCH OF SALT
- A PINCH OF SATAY SPICES

1. Spread the chopped cooked chicken over the sauce. Brush the chicken with pizza sauce. Top with some sliced red and green peppers. Sprinkle with grated cheese, and decorate with a mushroom.
2. Bake for 12 to 15 minutes at 220°C (425°F). After baking, season with satay spices, pepper and salt.

AUBERGINE TART

- 1 AUBERGINE, DICED
- 1 CLOVE OF GARLIC
- 5 TSP OLIVE OIL
- A PINCH OF GROUND BLACK PEPPER
- A PINCH OF SALT
- 100 G (3.5 OZ) MOZZARELLA, DICED
- 1 TBSP DRIED BASIL
- 50 G (1.76 OZ) GRATED EMMENTAL CHEESE

1. Fry the diced aubergine with the minced garlic in olive oil until tender. Season with salt and pepper.
2. Spread the aubergines on the pizza sauce, and top with the mozzarella cubes. Season generously with basil, and sprinkle with grated Emmental.
3. Bake for 12 to 15 minutes at 220°C (425°F).

ANCHOVY TART

- 2 LARGE TOMATOES, CUT INTO THICK SLICES
- A PINCH OF GROUND BLACK PEPPER
- A TIN OF ANCHOVY STRIPS IN OLIVE OIL
- 50 G (1.76 OZ) GRATED EMMENTAL CHEESE

1. Arrange the tomato slices on top of the pizza sauce. Season with pepper and add the anchovies in 3 rows.
2. Sprinkle with grated emmental.
3. Bake for 12 to 15 minutes at 220°C (425°F).

DELICIOUS SAVOURY BAKES

CHICKEN CURRY TART

- 200 G (7.1 OZ) COOKED CHICKEN, CUT INTO PIECES
- 100 G (3.5 OZ) PIZZA SAUCE
- 50 G (5 TBSP, 1.76 OZ) PINEAPPLE CHUNKS
- 20 G (2 TBSP, 0.71 OZ) COCONUT POWDER
- HOT CURRY POWDER
- 40 G (1.41 OZ) GRATED EMMENTAL CHEESE

1. Arrange the chopped cooked chicken on top of the sauce. Spread some more pizza sauce over the chicken, and top with the pineapple chunks.
2. Add a generous amount of coconut and curry powder to taste. Sprinkle with the grated Emmental.
3. Bake for 12 to 15 minutes at 220°C (425°F).

HAWAII TART

- 1 LARGE TOMATO, SLICED
- A PINCH OF GROUND BLACK PEPPER
- A PINCH OF SALT
- 5 TSP OLIVE OIL
- 200 G (7.1 OZ) HAM CUT INTO NARROW STRIPS
- 50 G (1.76 OZ) GRATED EMMENTAL CHEESE
- 100 G (3.5 OZ) PINEAPPLE CHUNKS
- A PINCH OF GINGER POWDER

1. Arrange the tomato slices on top of the pizza sauce. Season with salt and pepper, and drizzle with olive oil. Add the ham strips, sprinkle with grated Emmental, and garnish with pineapple chunks.
2. Bake for 12 to 15 minutes at 220°C (425°F). Season with ginger powder after baking.

CHAUSSON

MAKES 4 CHAUSSONS

- 600 G (21 OZ) PUFF PASTRY (SEE PASTRY BASICS, P. 24)
- 1 BEATEN EGG

The *chausson* is related to the South American *empanada* and the Middle Eastern *sambousek*. A great example of world cuisine! You can customise the recipe to your taste with the different types of fillings.

1. Line a baking tray with baking paper, and preheat the oven to 215°C (415°F).
2. Roll out the puff pastry with a rolling pin into a rectangle measuring 30 × 60 cm (1.181 × 23.62 in) and 2.5 mm (1/10 in) thick. Prick it generously with a fork.
3. Cut eight Ø 15 cm (5.90 in) discs from the rectangle. Place four discs on a baking tray. Lightly brush the edges with the egg wash, and spoon the filling of your choice into the centre (see below) (75 g (2.7 oz) of filling for each *chausson*).
4. Cover with a puff-pastry disc, and pinch the edges well. Brush the dough with the egg wash. Press your index finger into the edge, and use the blunt side of a knife to score the *chausson* from corner to corner. Poke your scissors into the dough a few times. This will allow steam to escape from the crust when baking. Let rest for half an hour.
5. Bake the *chaussons* for about 20 minutes.

DELICIOUS SAVOURY BAKES

FRIED MINCE, ONION AND HERBS

- 100 G (3.5 OZ) ONION, FINELY CHOPPED
- 3 TBSP OLIVE OIL
- 300 G (10.6 OZ) BEEF MINCE
- A PINCH OF GROUND BLACK PEPPER
- A PINCH OF SALT
- A PINCH OF FOUR-SPICE POWDER (SEE GLOSSARY, P. 32)
- A PINCH OF CAYENNE PEPPER

1. Fry the onion in some olive oil.
2. Add the mince, and stir while frying. Season with pepper, salt, a pinch of four-spice powder and cayenne pepper. Set aside to cool.
3. Spoon the filling into the centre of the chausson (see main recipe, steps 3 and 4).

MUSHROOMS

- 75 G (2.7 OZ) MUSHROOMS
- 1 CLOVE OF GARLIC
- 30 G (3 TBSP, 1.06 OZ) OLIVE OIL
- 250 G (8.8 OZ) CHEESE SAUCE (SEE PASTRY BASICS, P. 26)
- SOME CHOPPED CHIVES

1. Fry the mushrooms and the minced garlic in some olive oil, and leave to cool.
2. Stir into the cheese sauce with the chives.
3. Spoon the filling into the centre of the *chausson* (see main recipe, steps 3 and 4).

SPINACH AND FETA CHEESE

- 200 G (7.1 OZ) SPINACH
- 100 G (3.5 OZ) FETA CHEESE
- A PINCH OF GROUND BLACK PEPPER
- 1 CLOVE OF GARLIC
- 20 G (0.71) SESAME SEEDS

1. Bring water to the boil. Add the spinach to the boiling water. When the water is at boiling point again, blanch the spinach for another minute. Transfer the spinach to a colander, and drain. Squeeze out excess water with your hands.
2. Coarsely chop the spinach. Put into a bowl, and stir in the crumbled feta. Season with pepper and some minced garlic.
3. Spoon the filling into the centre of the *chausson* (see main recipe, steps 3 and 4).
4. Sprinkle some sesame seeds on the brushed *chausson*.

LOBSTER

- 250 G (8.8 OZ) CHEESE SAUCE (SEE PASTRY BASICS, P. 26)
- 45 G (1.59 OZ) LOBSTER MEAT
- 5 G (1 TSP, 0.18 OZ) CONCENTRATED TOMATO PUREE
- A PINCH OF CAYENNE PEPPER

1. Mix all the ingredients for the filling, and season with a pinch of cayenne pepper.
2. Spoon the filling into the centre of the *chausson* (see main recipe, steps 3 and 4).

SHRIMP OR SMOKED-SALMON FLAKES

- 220 G (7.8 OZ) CHEESE SAUCE (SEE PASTRY BASICS, P. 26)
- 80 G (2.8 OZ) BROWN-SHRIMP OR SMOKED-SALMON FLAKES
- 5 G (2 TSP, 0.18 OZ) CHOPPED PARSLEY

1. Mix everything together for the filling.
2. Spoon the filling into the centre of the *chausson* (see main recipe, steps 3 and 4).

BRIOCHE PISSALADIÈRE

SERVES 4

- 200 G (7.1 OZ) SALTED BRIOCHE DOUGH (SEE PASTRY BASICS, P. 26)
- 150 G (5.3 OZ) PIZZA SAUCE (SEE PASTRY BASICS, P. 27)
- 50 G (1.76 OZ) ANCHOVY STRIPS IN OLIVE OIL
- 50 G (1.76 OZ) RED ONION, SLICED INTO RINGS
- 50 G (1.76 OZ) GROUND PARMESAN CHEESE
- A PINCH OF GROUND BLACK PEPPER

Recapture that holiday feeling with this lovely pissaladière, a traditional flatbread from the south of France, with onion, tomato, anchovies and Parmesan cheese. This dish was very popular with fishermen after a day at sea because it was so tasty and filling.

1. Line a baking tray with baking paper, and preheat the oven to 230°C (450°F).
2. Knead the salted brioche dough, shape it into a ball, and let it rest for 30 minutes.
3. Using a rolling pin, roll the dough into a round disc Ø 20 cm (7.87 in). Transfer the dough to the baking tray. Spread with pizza sauce. Decorate the dough with anchovy strips in the shape of lozenges, add the onion rings, and leave to rise for 60 minutes.
4. Sprinkle the pizza with Parmesan cheese, season with pepper, and bake for 10 to 12 minutes.

GARNISHED QUICHE (*QUICHE GARNIE*)

Everyone knows these savoury tarts: a dough base with an egg-and-cream filling to which vegetables, meat or fish, and usually cheese are added. Here again, many variations are possible. For this book, I made the quiches even more delicious by adding a fun garnish after baking.

BASIC RECIPE; SERVES 6
- 200 G (7.1 OZ) SALTED BRIOCHE DOUGH (SEE PASTRY BASICS, P. 26)
- 100 G (3.5 OZ) GRATED EMMENTAL CHEESE
- 125 G EGG (2 ½ LARGE EGGS, 4.3 OZ)
- ½ G GROUND WHITE PEPPER
- 4 G (1 TSP, 0.14) SALT
- 140 G (⅗ CUP, 4.9 OZ) CREAM (40% FAT)

1. Lightly grease a tart tray with removable bottom (10 × 36 cm (4 × 14.5 in) and 2.5 cm (4 in) high) or a round tart tray with removable bottom (Ø 20 cm (7.87 in) and 2.5 cm (1 in) high) with butter. Preheat the oven to 200°C (400°F).
2. Make the salted brioche dough. Roll it out with a rolling pin. Form a rectangle (14 × 38 cm (5.52 × 15 in)) or a round disc (Ø 23 cm (9.05 in)). Push the edges up well with your thumbs to prevent the batter from overflowing.
3. Sprinkle grated cheese on the bottom. Beat the eggs and the spices, stir in the cream, and pour the filling over the cheese.
4. Finish the quiche to your liking (see below), and bake for 30 to 40 minutes.

SPINACH AND CHORIZO QUICHE

- 200 G (7.1 OZ) FROZEN LEAF SPINACH OR FRESH LEAF SPINACH
- 200 G (7.1 OZ) SLICED SPICY CHORIZO
- 25 G (3 TBSP, 0.88 OZ) COARSELY GRATED PARMESAN

1. Finely chop the leaf spinach, steam for a few minutes, and leave to cool. Or thaw frozen leaf spinach, which does not need to be steamed. Squeeze the moisture out of the spinach, and sprinkle the spinach over the filling.
2. Arrange the chorizo slices on top of the spinach.
3. Bake the quiche for 30 to 40 minutes in a 200°C (400°F) oven. Garnish with grated Parmesan cheese.

HAM, BROCCOLI AND BRIE QUICHE

- 100 G (305 OZ) COOKED HAM
- 150 G (5.3 OZ) BROCCOLI
- 200 G (7.1 OZ) BRIE CHEESE
- 20 G (3 TBSP, 7.1 OZ) FLAT-LEAF PARSLEY

1. Cut the ham into small strips, and sprinkle on top of the filling.
2. Cut the broccoli into small florets (no need to blanch them), and sprinkle them over the ham.
3. Cut the Brie into 3 × 4 cm (1.18 × 1.58 in) slices, and arrange on top of the broccoli.
4. Bake the quiche for 30 to 40 minutes in a 200°C (400°F) oven and garnish with flat-leaf parsley.

DELICIOUS SAVOURY BAKES

SALMON, LEEK AND PECORINO QUICHE

- 150 G (5.3 OZ) LEEK
- 200 G (7.1 OZ) SMOKED SALMON
- 100 G (3.5 OZ) FINELY GRATED PECORINO
- 10 G (1 TBSP, 0.35 OZ) DILL AND 10 G (1 TBSP, 0.35 OZ) EXTRA FOR THE GARNISH

1. Cut the leeks into 1 cm (0.39 in) wide rolls, and blanch for 3 minutes. Drain well in a colander, and sprinkle the leeks over the filling.
2. Flake the salmon, add it to the leeks, and sprinkle with the cheese. Finely chop the dill and sprinkle it on the cheese.
3. Bake the quiche for 30 to 40 minutes in a 200°C (400°F) oven. Garnish with some coarsely chopped dill.

SALMON AND BROCCOLI QUICHE

- A PINCH OF CAYENNE PEPPER
- 150 G (5.3 OZ) SMOKED SALMON FLAKES
- 200 G (7.1 OZ) SMALL BROCCOLI FLORETS
- 10 G (2 TBSP, 0.35 OZ) DILL

1. Season the quiche filling with a pinch of cayenne pepper.
2. Sprinkle the salmon on top of the filling, and add the broccoli.
3. Bake the quiche for 30 to 40 minutes in a 200°C (400°F) oven, and garnish with coarsely chopped dill.

QUICHE LORRAINE

- 2 ONIONS
- SOME BUTTER
- 100 G (3.5 OZ) OF LIGHTLY SMOKED BACON STRIPS
- 100 G (3.5 OZ) HAM, CUT INTO STRIPS
- 75 G (2.7 OZ) GRATED EMMENTAL CHEESE

1. Dice one onion, fry it with some butter, and leave to cool.
2. Mix the meat with the onion, and add to the filling.
3. Slice the second onion into rings, arrange the rings on top of the filling, and sprinkle with the grated cheese.
4. Bake the quiche for 30 to 40 minutes in a 200°C (400°F) oven.

BACON, CHERRY TOMATO AND ROQUEFORT QUICHE

- 150 G (5.3 OZ) LIGHTLY SMOKED BACON
- 125 G (4.5 OZ) SEMI-SUNDRIED CHERRY TOMATOES + AN ADDITIONAL 25 G FOR THE GARNISH
- 75 G (2.7 OZ) ROQUEFORT CHEESE, CUT INTO CUBES
- 10 G (2 TBSP, 0.35 OZ) MINCED CHIVES

1. Arrange the bacon on top of the filling, and add the cherry tomatoes.
2. Add the cubed Roquefort.
3. Bake the quiche for 30 to 40 minutes in a 200°C (400°F) oven, and garnish with tomatoes and chives.

POTATO-AND-HAM QUICHE

- 150 G (5.3 OZ) POTATOES
- 100 G (3.5 OZ) LEEK
- 100 G (3.5 OZ) HAM
- 1 CLOVE OF GARLIC
- 20 G (0.71 OZ) GRATED EMMENTAL CHEESE

1. Peel the potatoes, and boil them until they are almost soft. Set aside to cool.
2. Cut the leeks into 1 cm (0.39 in) wide rolls. Blanch for 3 minutes, and drain well in a colander. Set aside to cool.
3. Chop the ham, mix with the leeks, and season with minced garlic. Spread on top of the filling.
4. Slice the potato, arrange it on the filling, and sprinkle with the grated cheese.
5. Bake the quiche for 30 to 40 minutes in a 200°C (400°F) oven.

COLOPHON

Recipes
Stefan Elias

Historical introduction
Greet Draye (CAG)

Translation
Sandy Logan

Editing
Xavier De Jonge

Photography
Piet De Kersgieter
Séverine Lacante (p. 10)

Art direction
Natacha Hofman

Project management
Stephanie Van den bosch

Design
Tim Bisschop

Printing & binding
die Keure, Bruges, Belgium

Our thanks go out to everyone who has put their heart and soul into this baking book. In particular, we would like to thank Natacha Hofman and Stephanie Ryckaert, as well as Pots&things (Instagram: Lovepotsandthings) for the ceramics.

Publisher
Gautier Platteau

ISBN 978 94 6494 152 4
D/2024/11922/59
NUR 440

© Hannibal Books, 2024
www.hannibalbooks.be

The Centre for Agrarian History (CAG) is the knowledge centre for agrarian heritage in Flanders and Brussels. CAG studies the history and heritage of agriculture, food and rural life from the mid-eighteenth century to the present day.

www.cagnet.be

All rights reserved No part of this publication may be reproduced or transmitted in any form or by any means, electronic or mechanical, including photocopy, recording or any other, information storage and retrieval system, without prior permission in writing from the publisher.

Every effort has been made to trace copyright holders for all texts, photographs and reproductions. If, however, you feel that you have inadvertently been overlooked, please contact the publisher.

This publication has been compiled with the utmost care. Neither the author nor the publisher accepts any liability for possible inaccuracies and/or omissions in this edition.

PHOTO CREDITS

Front and back cover
© Piet De Kersgieter

P. 10
© Séverine Lacante

P. 12
Austrian Archives (S) / brandstaetter images / picturedesk.com

P. 15
Getty Images

All other photos
© Piet De Kersgieter